Rain Delay

Untold Stories from the Legends of Golf

Mark E. Squire

RAIN DELAY
Productions, LLC

Rain Delay Productions, LLC
www.RainDelayProductions.com
www.untoldgolfstories.com

ISBN13
978-0-9997175-0-9
"Rain Delay - Untold Stories from the Legends of Golf"

****

*"Golf is deceptively simple and endlessly complicated;
it satisfies the soul and frustrates the intellect.
It is at the same time rewarding and maddening
and it is without doubt the greatest game mankind has
ever invented."*

Arnold Palmer

****

Table of Contents

* Denotes interview information
supplied by Arizona Golf Radio

Foreword

By the time this book is completed, it will be just over two years in the making and lots of research, interviewing and writing has gone on over that time. However, what is more interesting, and sobering, are the lives that have passed during this period. We have lost individuals that define their eras, such as, Arnold Palmer, Prince, David Bowie, Alan Rickman, Gene Wilder, Leonard Nimoy, Debbie Reynolds and Carrie Fisher, to name just a few. I could fill many pages if I tried to mention them all.

Every generation will have its specific legends. The sporting arena, in this respect, is similar to movie stars and musical artists. We hear about these legends almost daily but we never really understand who they are or what makes them tick.

I've been extremely fortunate in my career to be able to sit with some of the most famous athletes in this country and listen to the stories they tell. Normally, this is in a private setting after a Pro-Am golf event or at an evening dinner presentation, where they are the speaker. Either way, only that immediate audience will ever hear these anecdotes.

In this book, these legends, or soon-to-be-legends, of golf reveal their antics, their stories and their challenges that make them more akin to us than you would ever think.

How Jack Nicklaus shanked a ball off the twelfth tee at the Masters in Augusta that almost took out Bobby Jones or how Fred Couples duffed a ball off the tee that bounced, sadly, into the water just ahead off the tee box. Doesn't that remind you of something you might have done at some time?

Mark E. Squire

They faced the same challenges growing up as we did; they simply took a different path. Gary Player stated, "Trevino was fantastic, you know, and his happiness was contagious. He always had great stories to tell, and this is one of the things I've tried to do with all this traveling around the world, to prioritize all the great stories I've heard. I've done a lot of after-dinner speaking and it's a wonderful thing to recall all these great stories. You'd better be sure to write them down."

That's what I wanted to achieve with this book, to be a historian, if you will. I wanted to make sure we never forget what made these players the people they are today before it's too late and they are gone forever.

****

"Reverse every natural instinct and do the opposite of what you are inclined to do, and you will probably come very close to having a perfect golf swing."

Ben Hogan

****

Acknowledgments

This book has certainly taken some twists and turns during its conception, but I'm happy to say that there are a few important individuals who made the book-writing experience the pleasure I always imagined it should be.

I've been extremely fortunate to have made many friends along the way, and none as important as Tom Lehman. It would have been really tough to introduce myself to so many noted golfers. After all, to them, who is this Mark Squire guy? Tom's introductions certainly helped pave the way to making this book a reality and are a great indication of just how popular and respected he is. Tim Cleary of Elevate Phoenix falls into this category too, and the work he's carried out with the kids at Elevate Phoenix is priceless.

The golfers themselves embraced this book and supplied stories the likes of which I thought I'd never hear. I feel very privileged to be in their company and they have treated me with utter respect. The stories vary so greatly and show what an amazing group of guys they are as well as the diversified backgrounds they come from. Ian Woosnam's reaction is still so clear in my mind. When I asked him if there were any stories he could tell me about his golfing career he said, "Are there stories? ****(expletive), yeah!"

I met Uncle Buck (Mike Rafferty) and Dan Pohl of Arizona Golf Radio during the final Champions Tour event of 2016, the Schwab Cup at Desert Mountain, Scottsdale, in Arizona. We discussed the book as well as the few issues I was facing in finalizing the stories. Sadly, my hopes for interviewing "The

King", Arnold Palmer, were dashed with his sad passing, but Mike came to the rescue. He gave me access to interviews that had taken place with Arnold and other golfing greats, giving the book its final lineup of participants. The information he supplied and the impact of the stories he made available on this book cannot be ignored.

As I discovered, and let me remind you that this is my first book-writing experience, it is vital to find a comfortable space in which to concentrate on what you are writing. My space, as it turned out, was Tempo Urban Bistro and Coffee Bar. I could sit down in the coffee bar, transcribe interviews, make my notes and write the stories while drinking great coffee, having pleasant distractions and eating wonderful food. The owners, Steve and Karen Maynard, followed the book's progress and loved the fact that it took place on their premises. I have to admit that I gave them a few snippets of information to see how they, as nongolfers, would react to the stories. Also, their premises are in the golfing community of Verrado, in Buckeye, Arizona, and that allowed me access to avid golfers who shared the same enthusiasm for the book. I quickly knew I was on the right track!

My copy editor, Sonia Castleberry, did a great job of reining in my unique Britishness, for want of a better word, and edited the stories, not content, for the U.S. market. She gently pushed me in a certain direction in respect to verbiage while at the same time complimented me on my work. When I submitted last stories to her, she made a statement that blew my mind. She said, "I didn't really get the vision you originally had, but after reading your stories I understand what you're doing. You've managed to get stories from like-minded individuals but retained their own identity and character in what they told you. I completely get it now." This is the biggest compliment anyone could have given me and really helped push the project across the finishing line. When you read Tom Lehman's chapter and his conversation with Fred Couples, you'll get what I mean.

Finally, "Traveling" Joe Passov, senior editor and writer for *Golf Magazine*, carried out five of the interviews and gave great advice throughout this project. He helped make sure I stayed true to the spoken word and gave direction when needed. He also introduced me to his sister, photographer Lori Kavanaugh, who, together with the participating golfers, other great photographers and business associates I made relationships with over my many years of golf photography, supplied a number of the images I was missing from my library. The book would have certainly been incomplete without them. Thank you all.

****

*"Columbus went around the world in 1492.
That isn't a lot of strokes when you consider the
course."*

Lee Trevino

****

Introduction

by John Spensieri

It began with this simple question: "Is there a reason why we don't celebrate our history at Phoenix Country Club, meaning the history of our past champions, who are the legends of golf?" After all, Phoenix Country Club had hosted the Phoenix Open from 1932 through 1986. And that's how it all started, how our History Week was born.

We chose our candidates each year, picking only from the past champions of the event, starting with Miller Barber, moving from Tom Purtzer, Dale Douglass and Kenny Venturi to Calvin Peete, Hal Sutton and Lanny Wadkins. Many people form their own opinions of these guys but you learn, very early on, to form your own opinion once you meet them. I've been extremely fortunate to stand shoulder to shoulder with these men, and I am blessed to now call these individuals my friends. I miss Kenny Venturi dearly, and Calvin Peete was just the sweetest man in the world.

To have these friendships on the Legends Tour and to understand these individuals, who are just like us but play the game that we love to a level that we can only dream of, is very special indeed. I see them now, in their later careers, acting so gracefully and graciously when they meet their fans, either at the driving range or in their pro tournaments, and representing the sport in the best way possible. It's a real treat to be around them.

To quote Bernhard Langer, "We're entertainers now," and having the opportunity to be around them in the same room, sitting down and having a drink with them, it's such a privilege. There are great stories that go along with each and every one of them. When we brought in Miller Barber, such a gentleman, our History Week wasn't as big as it is now. Miller didn't play because of a shoulder injury, but he wanted to go out on the course while the pro-am was going on. I had a girl by the name of Chelsea drive him around in a golf cart. She was very pretty and wore this little pink dress. I introduced her to Miller, and he looked up at her from the golf cart and said, "Chelsea, you and me gonna get along just fine today!" Later in the day I'm at the sixteenth hole and Miller and Chelsea pulled up in the cart. I asked Chelsea if he was doing okay and Miller if she was looking after him, joking with him by asking if her hands were in the right place. He snapped back, "No, they are not!" A smile beamed across his face. After play had finished Miller was gracious enough to sit for the entire dinner and made time to talk to anyone who approached him. He was the last one to leave the club that night.

I remember going up to see Miller on numerous occasions when he wasn't well, and I've become good friends with his wife, Karen, and their two boys, Richard and Larry. Karen is a sweetheart and recounted the story that Miller would tell about the time Phil Mickelson came to see him shortly before Miller passed away. Phil told Miller that he had a "better plan" for the U.S. Open, to be played at Merion Golf Club in Ardmore, Pennsylvania, that year, by hitting more four and five irons off the tee box, only for Miller to tell Phil, in his signature Southern drawl, "If you'd have hit more four and five irons off the tee box your whole career you would have won a lot more tournaments!"

****

*"Forget your opponents;
always play against par."*

Sam Snead

****

Hanging out with Kenny Venturi was always special, and I became good friends with him for the short time that I had to know him before he became ill, his trip to Phoenix Country Club being the last he took. I was so stressed because he didn't make a commitment to come to the club until after Christmas that year, and with the event in February, less than sixty days away, it was touch and go whether I could even find a replacement if he didn't make it. He did come to Phoenix, and when I picked him up from the airport he stated how happy he was to be here. I remember the night he did his one-on-one fireside chat with Curt Byrum. Our ballroom was packed and the crowd included Jay Feely, the then-current Arizona Cardinals placekicker, along with notables from other sports. The stories told that night were legendary, and members who had been at the club for forty-plus years still say it was one of the greatest events they'd ever had the pleasure to attend.

Kenny invited me and a couple of other individuals from the club to go back to his house to pick up some memorabilia for the club. I'll never forget the day three men in their sixties walked into Kenny's house in Palm Springs looking like three kids going to Disneyland for the first time! We were so excited that he invited us into his home, and a special presentation case now sits proudly in the

Calvin Peete

Phoenix Country Club's lounge area, along with souvenirs from other players, making our club so unique. While we were at Kenny's home, I noticed the beep of a smoke detector, and I asked him where it was. I was happy to take care of the problem so he could at least get a good night's sleep without that infernal noise we all know so well keeping him awake!

I became great friends with Kenny and his family, and he invited me to be part of the celebrations when he was inducted in the World Golf Hall of Fame, which was even more special as he entered under the auspices of the Lifetime Achievement Category. Unfortunately, Kenny didn't make the ceremony as he became deathly ill prior to the event. I keep in touch with his kids, Matt and Tim, and their children, play in Tim's annual charity event in Palm Springs and whenever I'm in California, I make a point to go and see Matt. Simply a great family, and I miss Kenny dearly.

I'll never forget the time Calvin Peete came to the club. We picked him up in this big limo—he loved riding in a limo—and took him to the Ritz Carlton. He called me the next day and said, "You know, I've got this friend in town who follows me around the country and I'm going to give him some lessons." I ask him where he was going to go and he replied, "I don't know. Some public course somewhere." I said, "Why don't you have him come to the club. I'll meet you there and we'll go out on the range." Calvin and I met the next morning in the pro shop, as it was a little chilly out, when he suddenly bolted out the door and walked to the first tee box. He was just standing there, and when I walked up to him, I saw he was crying. I said, "Calvin, are you okay?" He said, "Johnny, I've remembered playing this shot for years. I take it off that big tree and work it back. I know I can't reach the tree but I just draw it back into the fairway and you know, the only time I left these fairways all week was to go to the bathroom!" Calvin was a treat to have at the club, driving around with us on the golf cart, and I swear he spent time with everyone who played in the pro-am. We were very fortunate that he made it that day.

Mark E. Squire

Tom Purtzer, a local boy, was an honorary club member and just a great guy and, as Lanny Wadkins would say, "He still has one of the prettiest swings on the championship," while if you looked up the word gentleman in the dictionary, Dale Douglass' picture would be next to it.

Hal Sutton was another of these gentlemen, and I remember, like most people do, that classic battle he had with Tiger Woods and his never-to-be-forgotten quote, "Be the right club, today," while holding off Tiger to win his second Players Championship in 2000. At Hal's event we had fifteen other pros from the Champions Tour come in to play that day, with the majority of them showing up for the evening dinner. It was a great testament to the respect they had for a Ryder Cup captain like Hal, and what a great evening that was. Not only did Curt Byrum interview Hal that night but he was joined on stage by both Corey Pavin and Tom Lehman. The stories were coming fast and furious, and we all discovered what a great sense of humor these players had. Stories about the Ryder Cup ranged from Tom Lehman doing battle with a mumbling Nick Faldo to Corey Pavin and his sincere words about Bernhard Langer, "I learned the true meaning of the gentlemen competitor at the Ryder Cup from Bernhard Langer."

Fast forward a few days and I had the opportunity to walk with Bernhard at a practice round at the Champions Tour event down in Tucson. Bernard and I talked about the Ryder Cup and what it had become, with Bernhard wishing it would return to the friendly competition on the golf course that it used to be and not so much of a battle in the press as it is today. We walked and Bernhard played his practice round. After Bernhard completed the first nine holes, he turned and said, "John, I'm sorry for playing so slow." I replied, "Bernhard, this is the best nine holes

xviii

that I've never played!" Well, we are playing slow enough that the pair behind us, Larry Mize and Loren Roberts, had caught up to us. We all stood on the next tee box, a par three, and waited for the green to clear. Loren and Larry were talking to Bernhard when Larry said, "Bernhard, you missed this incredible dinner last night. We had no idea that Hal Sutton was so funny! He has amazing stories." It's incredible that these guys had such a great time and recounted stories the following day. They went there to honor a great player and had no idea that he had such a sense of humor.

It was great to have Lanny Wadkins at the club the following year. The members still tell me today how he took the time to talk to them about his career and showed a genuine interest in who the members were. I've had the opportunity to dine with Lanny on many occasions, but one time in Newport, John Mahaffey joined us and the stories started about how they grew up, playing golf in college and moving their careers into the professional arena. Turns out they had very similar careers, but neither of them knew it. Lanny is just incredible in that he can tell you about almost every shot he's hit in every tournament. It's amazing.

Phoenix Country Club started its own foundation years ago aimed at giving back to the inner city, where, in fact, the golf club is located. We have numerous charities and Elevate Phoenix has worked really well for us. It's a great charity for at-risk inner city kids, for getting them through high school and into college with the graduation rates for both high school and college through the roof. They are great kids, very respectful, and Elevate Phoenix does a great job.

****

"Golf is so popular simply because it's the best game in the world at which to be bad."

A. A. Milne

****

Section 1:
The Americans

CHAPTER

1

TOM
LEHMAN

One of my favorite weeks of the year has always been at the Westchester Country Club, a wonderful golf course situated just outside of Manhattan. There's just so much to do and my family would always accompany me there, leaving me to my golf, while they went and explored New York City. Year after year, I always seemed to play well and put together a run of really strong performances and finishes. In my view it was the perfect trifecta—a great course, a fun place and I always played well.

This particular year was no different and I got off to a good start, well up the leaderboard. Coincidentally, the NBA finals were taking place at the same time and the majority of the players on tour, myself included, are big sports fans. The Chicago Bulls and Michael Jordan were set to play that day in Chicago and Scott Simpson, who was good friends with Bill Murray, said he wanted to go to the game. He managed to get a hold of Bill and was invited to join him on his private jet, set to leave at four p.m., and go watch the game in Chicago. I said to Scott, "That sounds great. I wish I could go." Well, Scott put a call in to Bill and managed to get me an extra ticket to go to the game. I thought "Great, I'm playing with Scott, our tee time is at nine a.m. and we'd be done by one p.m. After the round we'd practice a little and be on the jet for four p.m. Perfect."

It didn't quite go as smoothly as I thought. At ten that morning, after completing nine holes, a big thunderstorm moved in and we found ourselves under a rain delay. It rained continuously, and soon it's eleven a.m. Scott and I were going crazy. We started doing the math and I said to Scott, "Okay, it's eleven a.m. now, so if we start at noon we'll be done by two p.m. We can still practice a little and make the flight." This soon turned into, "Well, Scott, it's noon now, but if we start by one p.m. we'll still be done by three p.m. and we can make the flight." Eventually, at two-thirty p.m., and with the rain showing no intention of letting up, I decided that we're not going to be able to make Chicago, but that's not what Scott was thinking. Scott turned to me and said, "Tom, I don't think we're going to get to play anymore today so I'm just gonna go." I replied, "Scott, how can you do that? How can you make that decision? This tournament is a great event and it's a really big deal. It could stop raining in fifteen minutes and we'd get our round finished by five p.m. If you leave and play resumes, you're going to get disqualified!" The whole time this was happening, Bill was on the phone telling Scott that he needed to make up his mind, they had to go. Scott made his decision and at just after two-thirty p.m. he was out the door and on his way to Chicago with Bill. As it turned out, the rain didn't stop and they canceled play for the day at around four pm. It worked out perfectly for Scott. He went to Chicago, watched an amazing basketball game with Bill Murray, flew back, and still got to finish his round the next day.

I was sponsored by Dockers at the time. The thing about that brand is that it's a very conservative, kind of an average, everyday working guy's product. So when Scott made the comment to Bill that I couldn't pull the trigger, that I didn't want to get DQ'd, Bill said, "Of course he couldn't pull the trigger, he wears Dockers!" I don't know of anyone else who would risk getting disqualified from a tournament to do what Scott did, but Scott is just one of those unique personalities. If it happens, it happens. There's always another week, another tournament. I'm not wired that way. The way I see it is that you can't give up on the week no matter what. Bill was certainly egging him on, after all, there's no big surprise, "He *is* a Docker's guy!"

In 1990, I was playing as an alternate on the Hogan Tour, known today as the Web.com Tour. The very first year there were five exemption spots to get a PGA tour card. I was an alternate member of the tour, which meant I was one of those alternates through July.

That July the weather in Wichita, Kansas, was typically hot and humid. Since I wasn't a full member on the tour, I didn't have a caddie assigned to me for that particular event. I went into the pro shop and asked if they had caddies available or if they knew of anyone who would caddy for me. Well, the course didn't have any caddies but the pro there knew of a couple of high school kids who occasionally came out. About an hour later he came up and told me he had a caddy for me and introduced me to this kid. His name escapes me, but I remember he had just finished high school and was a wrestler. He didn't know anything about golf, but I could steer him in the right direction and we soon had a system figured out. He carried the bag for me and basically kept me company, now and then throwing some grass into the air to let me know which way the wind was blowing. We struck up a nice little relationship and he soon became my teammate out there.

I shot a sixty-eight and then a sixty-six for the first two rounds, eventually finishing with a five under par to win the tournament and collect a twenty thousand dollar pay check, by far the most money I had ever made in my life. I saw it as such a blessing from above. I then thought about my current position: I was five thousand in credit card debt with no money in the bank. I was broke, trying to live on the week-to-week checks I got from the mini tour events, with a wife and almost newborn baby in the back seat of the car. This win was huge. Suddenly, I realized that I still had to pay my caddy, and when you win, you usually tip ten percent. I knew the guy had earned his caddy fee but did he deserve the extra two thousand dollars? After all, he just kept me company for the day and I could really use the money, but I decided that it was only what the kid was due. So, when I said goodbye to him I handed him two checks, one for his services and the other for his ten percent of the winnings. He

didn't look to see what he had in his hand, we simply said goodbye and parted ways.

About two months go by when out of the blue this two- or three-page letter turns up from this wrestler kid. In it, he went into his background and how he didn't want to talk to me about it as he didn't think it was his place. It was basically his life story. His dad had abandoned him when he was young and his mom had to work two or three jobs to provide for him and his siblings. She wasn't around much because of work and he started to mix with the wrong crowd, getting into trouble and drugs. While he was at high school he developed a relationship with his wrestling coach who got him a place at a Christian athletic camp where he started studying again. This coach got him back into wrestling and his life was really getting turned around when he caddied for me that day. He wanted to get a job so he could go to college after high school, but the college he wanted to go to was going to cost him two thousand dollars, and no one he knew had that kind of money. Turns out the check I questioned if he deserved or not was in fact what got him to college and paid for his tuition. It was one of those moments when you realize there's a bigger picture out there, and it's our actions that can affect lives in ways we could never imagine and vice versa. Life becomes a much more peaceful and successful path when people do the right thing. The world of golf can be so selfish in many ways, but when you understand this bigger-picture concept and do the right thing, you can change someone's life immeasurably. This kid knew to stay out of the way, determine the direction of the wind, when to speak and when not to. He became great company that day.

I took second place at the U.S. Open in 1996, but I just had to shrug off my round on the final Sunday. I was playing really well, but it was one of those rounds where I got practically nothing from the course. I shot a seventyone but played so much better. It just didn't happen. A bad bounce here, I just hit the down slope there and the ball rolled away from the hole, just the little things didn't go right. I wouldn't say it was bad luck, I just didn't get what I put in and ended up losing by a shot.

From there I went straight to the British Open, had bags of confidence, and was hitting the ball well. I was second in the world and had been for a while so everything was on an upswing for me, if you will. If I could just play my game, I'd have a real shot at winning this one. Everything looked good. I was playing a practice round with Fred Couples and his caddy Joe when I commented on how hard the course was playing. Fred looked at me and said, "This is hard? Nothing's hard for you!" It's amazing what people can say at times that can make such a difference. Unknowingly, he boosted my confidence through the roof.

****

"If a lot of people gripped a knife and fork the way they do a golf club, they'd starve to death."

Sam Snead

****

We start the tournament and I'm four under par through eleven holes on the first day, quickly into the lead and playing flawlessly. I can't remember if it's the twelfth or thirteenth hole on the course that is the easiest, with nothing but a five iron and sand wedge to the green with no trouble except bunkers off to the right. Of course, I hit my five iron, blocking it out to the right and straight into the bunker. I try to reach the green but put it right into the next bunker, following that by dropping it into the greenside bunker. I just blast out of that one only to two putt for a double bogie. I just doubled the easiest hole on the course and I was mad, smoking mad!

The last five holes were really difficult with the fourteenth, a par four, playing straight into the wind. I was always great on par fours and really roasted my tee shot up the middle of the fairway, following that with a laser-beam six iron to about eight feet. I've got a great chance for birdie, but I'm still angry. I mark my ball and don't just toss it to my caddy, I fire it at him. He catches it and knows that I'm mad. We're watching the other guys putt, and before he hands me the ball he snatches it away and says, "I just wanted to tell you that I'm caddying for the best player in the field." I made the putt, ending up with a sixty-seven on the first day, just one shot off the lead and eventually winning the tournament pretty easily, but it was that comment that brought me right back to the present. Not "That was a great six iron." It was "I'm caddying for the best player in the field" that got my mind turned around, and that's what makes a great caddy.

On the final Sunday of that tournament, since I was so highly ranked and one of the favorites going in, I was assigned a "placement", a security person if you will, a really big dude whose name, I think, was Kevin Boyles. He was about six feet four inches, and I would swear he played rugby. He had broad shoulders but was a real nice guy who went everywhere with me. I'm now playing the final hole and have a two-shot lead, hitting my tee shot left off the tee into a really nice position, and following it up with an eight iron onto the green. I could three putt and still win, a very stress-free situation. At this point everyone is rushing up the fairway and we get swallowed by the crowd. Kevin gets a hold of me with one arm and with the other just starts sweeping people aside to make way for me to get to the green. After I make my final putt to win the tournament he came over to me and said, "Tom, we've been through a lot of shit together, but now you're on your own!"

Andrew Martinez and Tom Lehman

The caddy/player relationship is really a team. It could be a two plus two equals three or a two plus two equals five thing. It could be a negative and detract from your game or a positive and add to it. The adding part for me has always been "Does your caddy say the right thing at the right time or does he give you what you need when you need it?" Andrew Martinez was my caddy for twenty-two years, from 1993 to 2015, and the relationship became way more about the friendship than the caddying. I would tell him, "The reason why you're still my caddy is not because you're a great caddy, which you are, but because I love you so much as a person. You're my dear friend."

My life as a regular PGA Tour professional really wasn't any different than any other of my contemporaries. I starting to travel while I was playing amateur golf and saw different parts of the country, then decided to turn pro after my collegiate and amateur careers. When I was sixteen, I saw my first golf course on the eastern side of the United States, The Country Club in Brookline, Massachusetts. I played in the US Junior Amateur Championship there, and that really opened my eyes to everything golf, from the history of the game and architecture of the courses to competition play.

It soon became obvious that I had an overwhelming love of golf courses and their architecture. They really are pieces of art. The courses I was able to study throughout my travels instilled in me a yearning for an education in golf in its entirety, its history, the courses I had visited, as well as the people who built them. That became my thesis. My friends were soon giving me a hard time when I went on field trips to see certain golf courses and would ask, "Why on earth are you doing that?" I would simply reply, "Well, I really enjoy it. I love it and find it interesting." I've always thought that someday I might use the information and expertise I had garnered from my field trips and education to provide an opportunity later in my career.

The first U.S. Open I played in was at the Hazeltine National Golf Club in Chaska, Minnesota. It was a young course that opened in 1962, and to say I was a bit green at that time would be a huge understatement. I had pretty solid rounds the first two days, despite the cold weather and strong winds, while other players, well above my standing, were suffering terribly. I was in fourth place, or something like that, and was invited to the press room, where one of the USGA executives asked, "Ben, will you carry or go through your round for the press here?" I agreed, took out my score card and confidently stated, "Four, five, four, five, four." Dan Jenkins and the other guys are laughing and the USGA executive said, "No, no. Let's see if you can describe some of your round." It was ridiculous, I was such an amateur!

When I think about that golf course, I really didn't find it that bad. However, there were some unbelievable comments in the papers, particularly from a guy named Dave Hill. He was a very combative guy, a fun guy but very combative. He said, "They ruined a good farm when they built this. All this place needs is eighty acres of corn and cows." You know, he caused quite an uproar. Dave finished second to Tony Jacklin that year, the only golfer under par at seven under, and the first Briton to win the U.S. Open since 1920, with John Mahaffey and myself tied for low amateur, meaning that we were invited to the acceptance speeches at the end of the tournament. After John and I had accepted our medals, Dave Hill, with his second-place finish, was asked to come up to the podium. As he walked up the crowd started booing and mooing like cows because of the comments he made earlier in the week, but Dave just got up there and yelled into the microphone, "If I could moo and boo, you bet I'd send you all back to the slaughterhouse!" John and I just looked at each other and I said, "God, is this what the Tour is like?"

****

"If profanity had an influence on the flight of the ball, the game of golf would be played far better than it is."

Horace G. Hutchinson

****

In 1971, I played in the amateur event at Wilmington Country Club, Wilmington, Delaware, which was my first trip to Pine Valley. I stayed with this guy at Wilmington who had attended graduate school at the University of Texas and knew a member at the club. One day he told me that we were going to play Pine Valley. I couldn't believe it and replied, "Oh my God, I've always wanted to go there." My first round there was very similar to many other people who play Pine Valley for the first time; it's usually your best. I shot sixty-seven that day and I haven't come close to it since. Even today that course still stands out as one of the all-time greats.

Playing in the Open at Merion that same year, I'm starting to understand these Eastern courses, and I remember how much I enjoyed studying and learning the different ways that people handle the land and how they route them. It was fascinating. Playing my first Masters in 1972, I finished tied for nineteenth place with the low amateur score. It was the first time I had seen Augusta, but I had read so much about it that when I actually got there it simply further fueled my appetite and interest in golf courses.

Moving on to April of 1995, and I'd just won the Masters for the second time, beating Davis Love III by one shot. I really didn't have time to enjoy the win as twentyfour hours later I found myself on Freeport McMoRan's plane, refueling in Hawaii, and heading halfway around the world to Indonesia. It was quite a bizarre situation, but I have to admit that when I returned from that trip the celebrations for winning my second Masters started and are still continuing today.

By this time my golf course business was in full swing, and Bill Coore, my partner of thirty-one years, and I were building a golf course, in conjunction with Freeport McMoRan's mining operations, for ex-pats working in Indonesia. There was another guy out there, Rod Whitman, who first introduced me to Bill, and we both think the world of him. Anyway, Bill and Rod were out on the course that was under construction, instructing the locals on how to use a rake. They had never seen a rake before, let alone know how to use it, as they were kind of slow coming into the twenty-first century at that time. There were about fifty workers raking for all their worth when this big monitor lizard slithers out of the jungle, and without missing a beat, they all dropped their rakes and caught a hold of this thing. They then proceeded to kill it, build a fire, cook it, and then eat it, right in the middle of what was going to be one of the golf course fairways! Bill and Rod burst out laughing as they couldn't believe what they had just seen. Bill said to me, "Well, I guess this is their culture and that's the way things work over here." It's crazy how primitive things are there and a million miles away from what I'm used to here in the United States.

I took another trip to Indonesia when the course was much further along but still under construction. It was literally built in a rainforest with upwards of three hundred inches of rain a year, meaning we'd have to dig trenches every twenty yards or so and backfill them with sand so that the course would drain properly. The trees are unbelievable there too, looking like matchsticks as they are incredibly thin but extend up hundreds of feet. They were barren on the bark with just a very few leaves at the top. Truly a weird but wonderful place to build a golf course.

During my career, I went to Japan on several occasions and was very, very good friends with Miller Barber, with whom I must have played a million practice rounds. Miller and Don January were two of my favorites and I really enjoyed my many rounds with them, but Miller was afflicted with so many illnesses, it was unbelievable. One morning during the Dunlop Phoenix Tournament in Japan, I had just woken up and poked my head out of my hotel room when Miller did the same, gestured to me and said, "Come here, come here." I joined him in his room where he asked, "Do you take allergy shots?" I responded that I had in the past administered my own shots, to which he said, "Well, you've got to give me my shot. My wife, Karen, is not here to do it for me." God bless him. Just knowing him, there was no one who complained more, and he must have been allergic to everything under the sun! He had this gigantic medicine kit in his golf bag that included every pill known to man, a bee sting kit, a snake bite kit, you name it, he had it, all in his golf bag. But I tell you, to go down there and give him his shot—that was wild.

The truth is, man, I really miss the guy. I miss him so much. He made me laugh more than anybody, he was just so funny. He didn't try to be funny; it was just the way he talked. You know, everything that could happen to anyone had happened to him, but he was such a loveable man and boy, could he play golf? Could he ever! One of the best.

Golf is a very social activity in Japan. It's a way to lose yourself from the hectic life the city provides and it means so much to them. They just love it. It's a real treat for them to be out in the country and the entire round, including lunch, is somewhat of a ritual. They play nine holes and then do all these other things during lunch, not only eat. They have a variety of entertainment and it's all very elaborate, eventually getting themselves back on the course to finish the back nine and their round. It really is quite the ceremony.

Jack William Nicklaus (January 21, 1940) is unquestionably golf's greatest champion. Every new star on golf's horizon continues to chase Nicklaus' record of eighteen professional major championships. He also captured two U.S. Amateur Championships, in 1959 and 1961, when they were considered majors. Among his other achievements are six Masters titles, five Player of the Year awards, and eight times the PGA Tour's leading money winner. Nicknamed The Golden Bear, Nicklaus also triumphed in eight Senior majors. He remains one of the game's most prolific and successful golf course architects with more than four hundred course designs in forty-five countries. Extremely active in charity work, Nicklaus was elected to the World Golf Hall of Fame in 1974 and received the Congressional Gold Medal in 2015.

The following selection of rarely, if ever heard stories, as told by Jack, spans his seven decades as a PGA Tour professional.

Arnold and I played in a pro-am prior to the 1968 PGA National Team Championship at Quail Creek Country Club in Oklahoma City, Oklahoma. Arnold was playing in one foursome while I played in another group. This guy who, I think, had something to do with the tournament sponsorship, drew me as his playing partner. I found out, however, that this guy had never, ever played golf before. He was so excited to play in my group that he was telling his friends, "Hey, I've never played golf before but I've got a chance to play with Jack Nicklaus!" With that he went to the pro shop, bought a set of clubs, and went out to hit some golf balls.

The next day we play the pro-am and we get to the third hole, I think it was. This hole is a little intimidating and we had a full line of people, each side of the tee box, extending down the fairway. It was this guy's turn to hit. He steps up and just whacks it, only to see the ball go straight into the crowd, hitting some guy right on the side of the head. We left the tee box to go and see if this poor guy was okay, and fortunately, he was fine. So, the group turns around to find our playing partner and let him make his apologies or something and he was nowhere to be found! He was gone! We never saw him again. Apparently, he was so mortified he just ran and left us.

While we're on the topic of pro-ams, I was playing in a pro-am event at Kapalua, on the beautiful island of Maui, where I was paired with Steve Gatlin of the Gatlin Brothers. Before we teed off, Steve's brother Rudy came up to me and said, "Jack, you're not going to believe it. This is Steve's first time that he's going out to play with you and he's a mess. He couldn't sleep a wink all night because he was so nervous. He actually got physically ill."

Knowing this, we all got up on the first tee and walked over to where we had our group photo taken. I put my arm around Steve and said, "Steve, I can't tell you how nervous I am. I didn't sleep a wink all night knowing I was going to play with you today." He turned to me with this look on his face as if to say, "You've got to be kidding me!" We all had a lot of fun and a great day together.

Jack Nicklaus and Arnold Palmer were friends and rivals for nearly sixty years. Not only did they pair to win PGA Team Championship and Ryder Cup matches, they also represented the United States in the Canada Cup (now the World Cup of Golf) on multiple occasions, winning the twoman team event four times as partners in 1963, 1964, 1966, and 1967.

In 1963, Arnold and I played in the Canada Cup. That event in Paris, France, where I also won the individual title, was shortened to sixty-three holes because of heavy fog. One day, the two of us were trying to get a taxi to take us back to our hotel while our wives, Barbara and Winnie, stood just a few yards away. We're standing there trying to hail a taxi when this guy walks around the corner. He looks at us and says, "Hey, you two guys looking for a little something? You don't want to get stuck with those two school teacher-types over there," as he looked toward our wives.

I turned to him and said, "Hey, those ladies are our wives!" Barbara and Winnie found it really funny and got a big kick out of it.

In February 2010, when Jack was opening his newest course design in Puerto Los Cabos, Mexico, his caddie was replaced on the first hole, an uphill par five, by a beerdrinking donkey that carried Jack's clubs up to the green. The donkey was rewarded with a cooling beverage of Sprite, as it turned out the animal's beer-drinking days had been curtailed. It turns out this wasn't Jack's first golf encounter with a donkey!

In 1966, I was in Las Vegas playing in the Sahara Invitational. I remember it well because, although the wind gusts topped out at about fifty miles per hour during my second round, it felt more like eighty miles per hour. I played the morning of that second day and shot seventyseven as the wind continued to blow.

That afternoon I decided to go fishing. I went with Herb McDonald, who used to run the tournament, and he commented how sorry he was about my round that day. I said, "I played like an ass. What's going to happen now? I guess you're going to have some junkie win your tournament." It wasn't a very kind statement toward another player but that was just how the conversation went. Anyway, as it happened, I shot a sixty-eight the next day and ended up winning the tournament with a final round of sixty-six. Herb had the last laugh, however, as at the final presentation he gave me a little donkey along with the winnings.

In the 1960s, Jack Nicklaus, Arnold Palmer and Gary Player were affectionately called golf's Big Three by their agent Mark

McCormack. Jack and Gary grew particularly close as they both had kids the same age.

In 1966, we took a business/family vacation to South Africa and spent time with Gary. Gary's brother, Dr. Ian Player, is a legendary conservationist and has a game reserve where he helped save the white rhino. After a tour of the game reserve, we went to a river to fish for tiger fish. There were crocodiles on the bank and in the river. The ones in the river, with barely their eyes out of the water, were just staring at us. Gary decided to take a nap on the river bank, while Ian, who couldn't give up the opportunity to have a good laugh, found a six- or seven-foot-long snake that just happened to be pretty darn poisonous. I couldn't believe it when he put it down right next to Gary and let it crawl over him while he was sleeping. When Gary woke up, there were some colorful words exchanged between the brothers.

Like Arnold, I also had an affinity for flying and we both became licensed pilots, but it wasn't all fun and games. I remember the first time I went to The Palmilla, flying into Cabo San Lucas, Mexico. I think it was 1963, and I was flying a Grand Commander with Stan Pierce, my pilot. I was lining up the runway, which just happens to be where the golf course is today. This runway actually went uphill, but I didn't figure on it going up by a factor of six percent, and as we were going into final approach Stan put his hand on top of mine and pushed the throttle forward. Well, what happens is that if you're lining up and using a runway that's going up six percent in elevation you think you're high but you're actually low! In fact, I was flying right into a cliff. Stan knew that he needed to increase the throttle as we landed. Thank you, Stan!

Mark E. Squire

"It took me seventeen years to get to 3,000 hits. I did it in one afternoon on the golf course"

Hank Aaron 1971

I'll never forget the first time I saw an "American twist" (read "kick") serve. I was playing at my house with Chuck McKinley, a former Wimbledon champion, and I thought I could play tennis, but as it turned out I was completely out of my league. He served a ball that moved to the right, hit the ground and moved back left, hitting me squarely between the eyes.

As a kid, I really thought I'd done pretty well. I was the nation's top junior, the best collegian and amateur player, and won the U.S. Open as a rookie on the professional tour, but that didn't stop my dad from keeping me grounded. He used to kid me all the time, especially if I'd played a round that wasn't very good, and made sure to get the next day's newspaper to point it out. Even if I shot a seventy-three or seventy-four he would point at the newspaper and say, "I see Stan Mosel shot a seventy-two" or he'd point out that Willie Mosely had shot a seventy. He liked to name these players in particular as he thought nobody knew who they were.

However, I happened to know Stan Mosel, and I knew Willie was an African American pro out of Detroit. I don't think my dad was aware that I knew of these guys, he just liked their names. So, this went on for years, and I have to say that Stan was a pretty good player who every once in a while would shoot a really good round.

My wife, Barbara, had heard this Stan Mosel reference for years. One night, when we were at the Waldorf Astoria hotel in New York for the Metropolitan Golf Writers Association dinner, Barb and I hopped in an elevator and were headed to our floor when it stopped . . . and none other than Stan Mosel walked in. I said to Stan, "Oh, hey, hi man, how you doing?" I then turned to Barbara and said, "Barb, Barb, this is Stan Mosel!" My wife could not hold it back. She remembered all the digs over the years and just burst out laughing. She couldn't help it and apologized to Stan for being rude, later admitting to me that she just couldn't help herself. She completely lost it.

To finish this chapter, I'd like to recount a couple of stories that have been told before. I'm sure some of the people reading this book might know them, but I'm sure some readers don't, so I hope they enjoy them.

It was my birthday, I was at Pebble Beach for the Bing Crosby tournament, and we were staying in a room right behind the eighteenth green at The Lodge at Pebble Beach. That evening we were in a room with about twenty other people when the phone rang. It was a friend of mine, John Swanson, from San Francisco. After wishing me a happy birthday, he said, "Hey Jack, I've got someone over here that wants to say something to you." I said "Okay, Swanny, whaddaya got?" Then this guy gets on the phone and starts singing "Happy Birthday" to me. There was so much noise in the room I didn't recognize the voice and when he finished singing, I very politely asked "To whom am I speaking?" He said, "Oh Jack, it's Bing Crosby. I just wanted to wish you a happy birthday but I guess I was a little hoarse." I just wanted to crawl under the table, I was so embarrassed!

The second of these stories is about something that happened with Arnold at the Bob Hope tournament. There used to be a jam session every day after play was over and during this one particular session, it just happened that Arnold and I went to the bathroom at the same time. As we walked out of the bathroom and back into the crowded room, I happened to brush up against this gal. I must have caught her hair between our shoulders as I pulled the wig she was wearing straight off her head. In a heartbeat, Arnold picked up the wig, put it on my head and we started dancing. Then I took it off my head and put it on Arnie's, and we carried on with our dance. The poor girl was mortified, but everyone found it funny and we all had a great time.

The first time I met Sam Snead we were paired together at the Greater Greensboro Classic in 1973. When I introduced myself to him on the first tee, he looked at me and said, "I know who you are, you're Hogan's boy." Almost thirty years later, shortly before Snead's death in 2002, I was visiting his nephew and good friend, J.C. Snead, at J.C's home in Virginia. During the visit, J.C. suggested that we pay a visit to "Unc," J.C's nickname for his famous uncle. When we entered Sam's home, J.C. announced that he had brought along a surprise visitor. Sam looked up and beamed, "Well I'll be, it's Hogan's boy."

My time at the Champions (Champions Golf Club in Houston, Texas,) was spent working in the golf shop, practicing and playing various mini tour events in places like Mexico, Atlanta and Florida. The next PGA Tour qualifying school was in the fall of 1971, and I was using these tournaments to keep a competitive edge while selling golf balls and posting tee times.

The Houston Champions International (now the Shell Houston Open) was a PGA Tour event that was held at the Champions from 1966 to 1971. As tournament week approached in 1971, preparations were in full swing. One day the pro shop was buzzing because we heard that Ben Hogan was coming in for some early practice rounds.

This was exciting. Hogan was nearing the end of his playing career and rarely played anymore. However, he had finished ninth at this tournament the previous year. I was hoping to meet him since I had actually learned to play golf by practicing the fundamentals he outlined in his book. I also hoped to get his autograph on my well-worn copy.

One evening after work, I received a telephone call from the pro shop asking if I would like to join Jimmy Demaret and Jack Burke, along with Ben Hogan, for a round of golf the following morning. Was this a trick question? I was a bit suspicious as Richard Killian, another assistant pro in the shop, loved to play practical jokes, so I was not sure if I should believe him but thought it best to play it safe and show up for the tee time.

The next day, on the first tee of the Cypress Creek Course at the Champions, I said good morning to my two employers and turned to look into the ice blue eyes of my idol, Ben Hogan. This day would change my life forever.

Hogan was slightly taller than my five feet, eight inches. For a small man he had large wrists and hands and powerful-looking forearms. He was dressed in a light blue golf shirt and gray pleated slacks. His custom-made black golf shoes were highly polished and he was wearing the white cap that had become his trademark. He was tan and lean with the look of a very confident man. He greeted me with a steely, piercing stare, extended his hand, and said, "Good morning son. My name is Ben Hogan." His handshake was firm and I noticed that his hand was hard, calloused and rough like someone who had done lots of manual labor.

Introductions done, Hogan, Demaret and Burke decided on a game that, given my financial situation at the time, would probably put me in debt forever if I lost. As the round progressed, however, I was totally unaware of the match as I couldn't take my eyes off Ben Hogan. I was in awe of the swing I had worked so hard to mimic. Hogan was literally a machine. He was sixty-one years old at the time and hit the ball as solidly as anyone I had ever seen. The sound of the club hitting the ball was different from any sound I had ever heard on a golf course. His ball flight was remarkable. To this day, I can still see the ball tracking like a laser beam against the grey Texas sky.

As we played on I became more relaxed and birdied the par three eighth and par five ninth. Unfortunately, the skies opened up as we walked off the ninth green, and thunderstorms chased us off the golf course for the day. We went inside to calculate the scores and, I thought, to settle up on the team match. I had shot thirty-two on the front nine. Hogan shot thirty-three.

Hogan huddled with Burke and Demaret in the corner of the locker room. Occasionally one of them raised his head and stared at me. I felt as though I had committed some heinous crime. Finally, Hogan walked over to me and said he would like to continue the game tomorrow if I could be available. I looked over to Burke and Demaret and they both nodded yes. What a thrill to play two days in a row with one's hero. Yes, I would be back tomorrow.

After a steady all-night rain, the morning brought overcast skies and strong, gusty, southerly winds. This would make the golf course play at its most difficult with the finishing holes directly into the wind. Again, I paid little attention to the team aspect of our match and concentrated on the individual game. The day dictated lots of pars sprinkled with a few birdies but very few bogies or higher. It proved to be a tough day with Hogan carding a two-under seventy to my one-under seventy-one.

We made our way to the locker room to tally up the results. I felt a bit out of place as the three of them again huddled by one of the lockers. After what seemed an eternity, Hogan walked over and said that if I came to the club for dinner, we would then settle up for the match. This was not an invitation to dine with him but a summons to be in the restaurant at seven p.m. I had no idea what to expect that evening and certainly did not know that it would change my life dramatically.

I was sitting in the dining room that evening, finishing my dessert, when Hogan walked in and approached my table. He came right to the point: "Son, would you like to play in the Colonial Invitational next week in Ft. Worth?" My reply, "Mr. Hogan, I'm not a member of the Tour," was met with his retort: "I didn't ask if you were a member of the Tour, I asked you if you would like to play Colonial next week." Sheepishly, I answered, "Yes sir, I would."

He disappeared into Jimmy Demaret's office for about fifteen minutes and then returned to where I was seated. He must have been a wonderful gambler because I could read nothing in his actions or expression. Then his face broke into a big smile and he said, "You are in." I could not believe it. Not only had I had two glorious days playing golf with Ben Hogan, but now I was playing in a PGA Tour event at Hogan's Alley, Colonial Country Club. His voice interrupted my daydream when he said, "There is one stipulation, however, you must play your practice rounds only with me." No way, I thought. Are you kidding me! This could not be real. But it was.

From that day forward, my golfing career was unmistakably linked to Ben Hogan. The man who unknowingly taught me to play golf through his book became my mentor, sponsor, and great friend.

****

"Golf and sex are about the only things you can enjoy without being good at."

Jimmy Demaret

****

I took up the game of golf relatively late in life at nineteen years of age and really never took it too seriously. I guess I was just meant to play it. I had a lot of talent but my swing was kinda unique, certainly no Sam Snead for sure. The confidence was oozing out of my pores, and it didn't matter when I turned up to play a round, whether I hit practice balls or not, I could just turn up, go straight to the first tee, and hit. It didn't make any difference. I could hit the ball within four seconds, having only looked at the target once. I didn't have to waggle the club and all that stuff. I was never going to get a slow-play penalty, that's for sure.

Which leads nicely to the 1990 U.S. Senior Open that I won at Ridgewood Country Club in Paramus, New Jersey. Jack Nicklaus, who I beat by two strokes, was playing in the group behind me and was consistently three holes back. I went up to the tournament official and told him that it wasn't right for Jack to be so far back all the time and that I was always waiting and couldn't get a rhythm going. He replied, "Well, Jack plays a little slower and needs a lot of time." That's the first time I had ever heard of it, so I asked, "What does that mean, exactly?" The official answered, "You get so much time for six holes, for four holes or whatever, and if you're behind we start timing you." I replied, "Oh, so you mean that if tomorrow I get to number eleven and I'm forty-seven minutes in front of my time I can just sit on that bench and wait until my time has caught up?" He said, "Well, there's an etiquette part to it here too." I said, "Etiquette, my ass. The man's three holes behind!"

I got my caddy, Herman Mitchell, from Miller Barber. When I first came on tour I had a couple of different caddies, but none of them seemed to work out, so one day I asked who was the best caddy out there on tour. Everyone gave the same answer— Herman Mitchell, who caddied for Miller Barber. I went to see Miller and asked him if I could approach Herman to work for me. Miller was more than happy. He said I was a much better golfer than he was and he wouldn't stand in the way of this opportunity for Herman. I approached Herman, who accepted the position, but he asked me if I had spoken with Miller first. I said I had and all was good.

Herman went to work for me, and I'll never forget our first tournament at the Pensacola Country Club in Pensacola, Florida. The hole was a dogleg right and I drove the ball but it didn't cut. Instead, it came to rest in the trees straight ahead. It wasn't too deep in there, but it was definitely a chip shot out. We went in and surveyed the situation, and then I asked Herman for the sand wedge. We were about one hundred and thirty yards out, and Herman asked me to confirm I was just chipping the ball out. I said, "No, I'm going to duck hook this ball onto the green." He said, "Lee, Lee, just chip it out." I restated, "No, I'm going to duck hook it onto the green." Well, I duck hooked it and put it on the green. Herman turned to me and said, "I can't club for you." I replied, "You're not meant to club me, you're meant to just tell me how far it is. That's all I need you to do."

Herman ended up being with me for twenty-seven to twenty-nine years. He was family to me and lived in my house on Jupiter Island, Florida. He drove a big old Cadillac, and when he got onto Jupiter Island the police would follow him home every night. They would follow him home thinking, "There's a black guy on Jupiter Island. What the hell's going on? You know nobody's cutting grass at this time of night!" Then they found out they had a Mexican living on the island too and thought the place must have really gone to hell!

✳✳✳✳✳✳✳✳✳✳✳✳✳✳

"I have a tip that can take five strokes off anyone's golf game: it's called an eraser."

Arnold Palmer

✳✳✳✳✳✳✳✳✳✳

The first time I went to Phoenix, I drove my sixtyfive Plymouth station wagon from El Paso, and I had to go to a golf course way up in the mountains where they were having this tournament. When I get to Phoenix I was told I had to go up into the mountains north of the city to this place, I think it was called Desert Mountain. After stopping for directions, I found myself going up Pima Road, and man, is it dark out there! I mean really dark, and you guys know me, I was always watching those John Wayne Indian movies and I was just scared to death going up there. I drove for what seemed like forty miles, and I don't see a thing, no lights, nothing, so I turned around and came all the way back to Phoenix. I told the guys who gave me directions what had happened, and they said, "Nope, you just didn't go far enough!" I finally got up there and played pretty good, making the quarter finals before losing in a match play event.

We loved coming to Phoenix; it was the best place in the world for us. We played at Phoenix Country Club, and that was simply a little darling of a golf course. It still is today. We used to go to the race track and watch those greyhounds run, and that was real fun too. I've got so many great memories of that place and that's as far as I'm going to go on that topic, before I get myself and others into some real trouble!

When I think about the Masters and Augusta, I have to admit that I've actually come to confession in the last four to five years about the place. I've come to understand that my issues were never anything to do with Augusta. I said that the golf course didn't fit my game as an excuse because I just couldn't stand The Dictator, a gentleman named Clifford Roberts, who served as chairman of Augusta National Golf Club from 1931. He and I had a run-in with each other the very first time I got there. We didn't see eye to eye on the ticket situation when he had my friends, even though they were in my automobile, get out and walk down to the other gate instead of simply coming in with me. I never understood why they had those sorts of rules when no other golf tournament had them. We just couldn't see eye to eye, and to tell you the truth, I wanted to whup him, but I just couldn't get to him!

After that one time he and I got into it, which was around 1970 or 1971, we just never talked, we never spoke to each other again. I didn't feel uncomfortable, I just didn't want to go in there and look at the man. I didn't go there for three years, until Jack [Nicklaus] talked me into going back. The fact that I wasn't playing there was never anything to do with Augusta or the golf course, and honestly, if you can play Augusta you can play anywhere. Back in those days, if they'd put up prize money we'd have played in the parking lot! It didn't make any difference, and it absolutely had nothing to do with Augusta.

I'll tell you a little story about when Mr. Roberts died. He actually killed himself, committed suicide they say, on a par three there. I don't quite remember which par three, but I do remember, as you just can't make this stuff up, he had just committed suicide and we turned up there for the tournament. I was leading after the first thirty-six holes, and everyone was asking about where on the course he was buried, but no one would give out that information. I went to the press room that Friday night and said exactly this, "You know, people have been wondering where Mr. Roberts was buried. You'll all be able to witness this tomorrow because when he finds out I'm leading this golf tournament there's going to be a big crack opening up in the ground from where he's turning in his grave!" I swear you could hear a pin drop in that press room it went so quiet!

The great thing about Augusta is that everyone is gutless who goes there, from the players to the media. They're walking on eggshells, and they're afraid they're going to say something wrong, afraid they're going to be in the wrong spot, absolutely scared to death! And when they go to the greatest golf tournament in the world, the USGA, the one that has promoted the game forever, they're the first to criticize everything. The food, the golf course, the putting surface, the air that they breathe, everything.

As everyone knows, I'm not a polished individual. When I get a grudge, it tends to stay there, but I've got a little better. I married a lady thirty-two years ago who softened me up a little bit. I wasn't a very social guy, and I believed in one way and one way only. It was very difficult for me to take people in and allow them to get close to me. I didn't do that very often. It's strange, in a way, because I've always been a talker. I've never tried to intimidate anyone with it, it's just something that I did. I guess I picked it up from my days caddying, you know, hustling a little bit. When I worked in the pro shop I could sell a size nine pair of shoes to a guy who was a twelve D, and he'd tell me they fit him perfectly. I swear I could sell ice cream in a blizzard in Alaska.

In the early eighties, at the Canadian Open at the Glen Abbey Golf Course in Oakville, Ontario, I was playing with Jerry Pate and Dan Pohl. Well, we start off and straight away it seemed like Jerry was trying to get into the joketelling business against me, and it wasn't going to end well for him. He finished up shooting an eighty-two that day, and we called him Jimmy Carter because he was always smiling like a catfish and nothing came out of his mouth worth a damn! He never stood a chance; I could get into a car and talk to the radio.

I once played with Tony Jacklin in the World Match Play semifinals, held at the Wentworth Club near London. We were walking up to the first tee when Tony walked by me. As he walked past he said, "Mex, Mex, just listen, I just want to say something to you today," I said, "Okay, what is it?" He replied, "Whatever you do today, don't talk. I don't want to talk today, I just want to play golf." I said, "You don't have to talk, just listen!"

I was talking about this story with a friend a few days ago, and I think it's a good one to finish on. Back in 1971 I lived on

Mark E. Squire

Ridgewood Ave in El Paso, Texas, about three doors down from
Tony Lama. I was in pretty good shape back then, at one hundred
and seventy pounds, not the plumpy little guy I am now. I was
out there in a pair of white shorts and sneakers, and the yard guy
was mowing the lawn while I was helping out a little by clipping
the Bermuda grass from the sidewalk with a hoe. Anyway, this
white Cadillac pulled up about three feet from me, and the lady
driving it lowered the window and asked, "Young man, do you
speak English?" I replied, "Yes, ma'am." She then said, "What do
they pay you to do the yard?" I smiled and said, "Well, the lady in
this house lets me sleep with her!" She just raised that window
back up and drove off.

This story goes all the way back to my earlier years, growing up with my dad and getting to know the ropes. Although, all the experience I garnered over the years would never prepare me for what happened in England in 1993.

My dad played for Harvey Penick, the golf coach at the University of Texas in Austin until 1963, and also played a few events on tour, the bigger tournaments mostly, but he knew he was always going to be a club pro. Harvey influenced him in everything golf, not only playing but how to be a gentleman of the game and my dad admired any golfer who had had a connection with Harvey, such as Tom Kite or Ben Crenshaw. Well, I picked up the game early and got to a pretty good level. My dad had gotten to be good friends with Tom over the years, so when I went on tour my dad asked Tom, "Would it be okay if Davis plays the practice rounds with you?" He was basically asking Tom if he could help a rookie kid out. Tom was more than accommodating and replied, "I would be happy to, as long as he's willing to work. He'd better show up with a yardage book in his pocket, on time and ready to go. We're not going to go out there and goof around." Tom took me under his wing and showed me how to be a tour player, although I was still a little nervous of being around such a great individual as he had similar traits to Bernhard Langer, very serious, just the opposite of me. It was the kind of influence I needed, and I played lots of practice rounds with him on tour.

I clearly remember my first Masters, barraging Tom with questions like how early are we going and when are we going to leave? And he's like, "The course doesn't get ready until Tuesday. Don't worry about it." I'd follow with, "Wait, I thought we were going to go like five times the month before!" I needn't have been concerned, I learned so much from him on how to be prepared for tournaments. For as long as we were together on tour, even the Champions Tour, he would always let me watch him give a lesson or watch him hit balls after a round or include me at dinner. Every time I see a kid on tour I don't really know, I try to make sure that I say, "Hi" or help out by joining him for a practice round or something, because although I'll never be able to give back all that Tom taught me, I can try. It was a great mentorship for me and I found myself included in his circle with the likes of Ben Crenshaw, Curtis Strange and Jay Haas. I was very lucky as a rookie.

****

"They call it golf because all the other four-letter words were taken."

Raymond Floyd

****

Moving on to that Ryder Cup in 1993. It was the thirtieth Ryder Cup and was held at The Belfry in Wishaw, Warwickshire in England. Everyone's trying to figure out their playing partners as you play the course based on alternate shots. I'm a good partner for Tom as I'm the long hitter and he's the wedge or putter guy. All the players do it, it's kind of a Ryder Cup thing, figuring out how many wedges or putts there would be in the round, who would hit off the even tees and who hits off the odds, and therefore, who would be your best partner. We get to Thursday when they announce the teams and sure enough, I'm paired with Tom Kite. We've got this figured out. Then we find out who we're playing, none other than Seve Ballesteros and Jose Maria Olazabal, and they've never lost.

Friday morning rolls around and I'm obviously nervous, but we find ourselves under a fog delay. We wait on the first tee, and we're standing with Jim Mackay, who everyone knows as Bones. He bought his own ticket to come over and help out as he figured he and Phil Mickelson would play a lot of Ryder Cups and he wanted to experience what it was like to be part of the team and to help out. Fred Couples was with us on the tee. We're all just standing around and Fred's leaning on my bag, pulling clubs out to look at these graphite shafts, which were pretty new back then, when the head of the nine iron comes clean off the shaft! It twisted and just comes right off. Great, my first Ryder Cup and my clubs are falling apart on the first tee. Bones, who's more the team mascot as he doesn't really have anything to do, runs off to find some glue to put the head of my nine iron back on. He comes back with the club repaired, and says, "It'll be ready in five to ten minutes, just don't hit any balls on the range with it."

After warming up, we walk around on this path that leads to the first tee, which is an odd hole, when I said to Tom, "I just figured out that number one is an odd hole, so I'll let you hit first." He stopped dead in his tracks and said, "No, no, no. No. We figured this out already, you're going to be fine." I had just panicked when I realized I was going to hit the first shot with Tom Kite against Seve and Jose Maria. Tom said, reassuringly, "Look, you're going to be fine. Just hit a one iron out there in the fairway. We're going to whup these guys." Sure enough, I got it off the tee and in the middle of the fairway, and we won the match. Unfortunately, we drew them again that afternoon, and they beat us.

So, my nine iron broke and the head was glued back on. I used it a couple of times that day, but a joke started going around that night: "Not only is Davis falling apart nervous, but his clubs are falling apart too!" How does this stuff happen? How does Rory McIlroy almost miss his tee time? Some weird things always happen at these big events.

I'm playing Constantino Rocca in the final singles match of the final day. We're at the seventeenth tee when Tom Watson and everyone else start turning up. He's nervous, I'm nervous, and he says to me, "Go get 'em. We really need this point." I reply, "Yeah, no kidding!" Now I'm nervous that he's watching me, so I say to Tom (but I was really trying to convince myself), "You know, he's due to miss a putt and I'm due to make one." Sure enough, Constantino misses his putt for par, and we head to the eighteenth. I hit a bomb of a tee shot, a three wood around the corner. I think it's the best three wood that I've ever hit, just bombed it over the lake and out of sight, way down there. And what club did I have for my final shot of the Ryder Cup? It's a nine iron! So I hit this nine iron, and it was a pretty good shot, but it went quite a way up the hill before spinning back to leave me with a four-and-a-half footer straight uphill for the win.

I got up to the green, and I was so nervous, my hands were shaking, I was shaking. I backed off and started my routine over again, this time striking a solid putt that went straight in the cup. I threw my hands up in celebration, and that image was captured forever. I looked at the ball in the hole and thought to myself, "Oh, it worked!" However, the true story behind that famous picture was more of the fact that the nine iron that Bones fixed during the fog delay on that first day had actually held up, and, of course, that we had won the Ryder Cup. Hey, I backed off, I was nervous, I did my routine, and I sank that putt after hitting that nine iron, the nine iron that held together.

Bones and I talk a lot about what happened, about him becoming our mascot that year. He's so passionate about his job, about the Ryder Cup and being prepared. This is something I tell the guys today. If you just miss out on the Ryder Cup team, you're going to make it eventually, come and watch the event and just be there for your team. The Europeans have done that in the past. Bones was there to support us, he was there when that nine iron broke and he fixed it. He was a team guy all the way, and when I went to hit that nine iron I just had to believe that Bones had taken care of it and everything was going to be okay.

So I had Kite and now Bones to go with this twentyyear-plus relationship of being on the Ryder Cup teams together. If anybody asks, "Hey, do we have enough towels" we know that Bones will go get them. He's the guy who always saves the day. Bones is always so calm and that's probably the reason he's lasted so long with Phil. He's like, "I got it." He just took off that morning like it was no big deal, he just gets things done.

Once, early in Phil's career, Bones was talking about what he wanted to do and he said to me, "Maybe I could work for you. Maybe I could work for Phil." He paused a while and then said, "You know, I've got a great opportunity with Phil. I'm going to stick with Phil." What a great choice for him and I've had the pleasure of being around that particular relationship for a long, long time. You just can't say enough about the passion our guys, as well as their caddies, have for the Ryder Cup. I remember when Phil and Bones came off the eighteenth hole at the President's Cup and looked for me to tell me that we were ready for the Ryder Cup." Bones built that relationship. He built it right then in that fog delay. He's a team member, he's a team guy.

****

*"The greatest reward in life is to be remembered.
Thank you for remembering me."*

Kenneth Venturi

****

My Memories, by Tim Venturi

I was only five years old when my father won the U.S. Open in 1964, but my brother Matt and I held him to a very special promise he had made us. He said that if he ever won the U.S. Open he would come back home and build us a swimming pool in our backyard. He kept his promise, and we spent many hot afternoons playing with him in that pool.

I had a really bad accident the next year. I was going down a very steep driveway on my bike and somehow managed to catch my mouth on a hook that was sticking out the back of a truck. It took the side of my face off, and the truck ran over my leg, putting me in hospital for six months. This happened when my dad was heading toward the latter part of his career, but I'll never forget how he kept my spirits up while I was in the hospital. He got some of his good friends to come in and visit with me, and these were some very special friends! Willie Mays visited on one occasion. On another day, John Brodie and half of the San Francisco 49ers showed up. The entire Warriors team even stopped by. My dad really went out of his way for me, calling on these athletes to come see me, and I always thanked my father for what he did.

We went to Bing Crosby's house the night before I was to go back to elementary school. I went to school with his two sons, Harry and Nathaniel, while Mary Frances Crosby, Bing's daughter, was my first girlfriend. We were all sitting at the dining table when Kathryn, Bing's wife, said, "Now Tim, you're going back to school tomorrow and all the kids are going to ask where have you been and what happened to your face? I want you to tell

them this. I want you to tell them that you are the great white knight saving the princess from the bad people."

As we were driving home that night, I asked, "Dad, what do you think about that story Mrs. Crosby told me to tell about me being a prince?" He looked at me and said, "Son, that lady is so full of it! When you go back to school you tell those kids you got hit by a truck and that's what happened to your face. 'Cause that's exactly what happened."

My dad taught me a lot and he never stopped teaching me this: You show a man how good you are, you don't need to tell him. My dad shared many things with Matt and me, and it was all great advice. I really respect him for that.

I traveled with him on tour for a couple of years and distinctly remember when I first arrived at Augusta with him. He said, "Okay son, I'll give you twenty-five cents for every weed that you can find." I thought I was going to make a killing, but I couldn't find one weed. I came back empty handed and saw the knowing look on dad's face. He knew it was a safe bet.

We moved to Palm Springs in the 1970s, where we hung out with one of my dad's best friends and my godfather, Frank Sinatra. I'm always very proud to have had Mr. S, as I called him, as my godfather. My dad originally came to Palm Springs to help open the Mission Hills Country Club, but soon after that his hands failed him and he couldn't play on the tour anymore. I was about twelve at the time and the house my dad was building wasn't quite ready, so Mr. Sinatra, being the extremely kind man that he was, said we could live in the cabana on his property until our house was finished. When I came home from school one of my jobs was to detail all of his cars and do a few other chores that needed seeing to. Those were really fun days with just my dad, myself and my brother living in that cabana. We had the keys to and the run of the entire house, and we'd go to the theater room and watch movies all the time. It was phenomenal!

After we moved into our new home, Mr. Sinatra and Jilly Rizzo, Mr. Sinatra's right-hand man, came by one day and said, "Ken, were going to take a little ride." They went to New York

City and dad didn't return for four days. What I think of most is that when dad left the house he didn't take anything with him—no clothes, luggage or anything!

I saw firsthand the pain my dad suffered as his hands began to deteriorate during the late 1960s. It was really tough for him as he started to miss cuts, and he'd come home early. The thing that impressed me was that although he'd missed a cut, he would still be just regular dad when he got home. He'd talk about other players, even though some of them didn't get along quite as well as today's players. He sometimes talked about the sad end to the life of professional golfer Tony Lema in 1966. My father and Tony were supposed to do a charity engagement, but Tony, the night before, chose to go to another function where he was going to be paid to appear as opposed to not being paid for the event with my dad. Dad told Tony that he was making a mistake, and he wished Tony wouldn't get on the plane. Unfortunately, Tony did get on that plane, and he lost his life when the plane crashed at Lansing, Illinois.

I recall the day when dad called Matt and me and said the producers of *Tin Cup* had approached him to play a part in the movie. He said he didn't want to do it but Matt and I said, "Dad, you've gotta do it! It's a *Caddyshack*. You gotta do the movie!" He took the part and even ended up teaching Kevin Costner how to play golf. He hadn't played before, but by the time filming was finished Costner was a two handicap. I love to watch my dad in that movie. I think it's the greatest golf movie since *Caddyshack*.

After the movie, they resurrected a book about my dad called *The Match*. It was written in 1956 about a match at Cypress Point when my dad and Harvie Ward, two amateurs from San Francisco, played with Byron Nelson and Ben Hogan, the game's greatest living professionals. That match became a legend in golf circles and is considered the greatest private match ever played. It tells so much about my dad's character. Read it, and you'll understand why he was so respected by Ben Hogan and Byron Nelson.

Tim (age six) and Ken Venturi

I have so many fond memories of my dad, but the story I'll leave you with is one of my favorites. Carroll Shelby built my dad a Shelby Cobra when he won the U.S. Open in 1964. When my dad came home on weekends he would take Matt and me out for a ride. Bearing in mind how young we were, this was just so much fun. He'd tell my mom, "We're going to go out for a ride in the Cobra," and we'd go out to the San Mateo Bridge. There was this long straightaway about fifteen miles out and he would say, "Okay boys, I'm going to blow the pipes out now." He'd get the car up to about one hundred and forty miles per hour, and while slowing down, he'd remind us not to tell our mother about it. Growing up with my dad and going out for rides in the Shelby Cobra, it was all a lot of fun. I grew up with a Shelby Cobra in the garage and now I'm fortunate to have one outside in my garage. Our family doesn't have my dad's Shelby Cobra anymore, but heard it sold some years ago for two million dollars, so much more than we sold it for!

My Memories, by Matt Venturi

I was about seven years old in 1964 when my dad won the U.S. Open and away at a sleep-away camp called Gold Arrow. Before I left for Gold Arrow he promised that if he won the event he would build us a swimming pool. It didn't really resonate with me at the time because I was so young, but when the camp counselor came running up to me saying, "Your dad just won the U.S. Open," all I did was run around to all my friends and tell them "Geez! I'm going to get a swimming pool now!" That was a really good feeling, but it must have been nothing to what my dad was experiencing.

The first car he bought after winning the Open was an Aston Martin DB4. It was red with a tan leather interior—a really beautiful car. Then we got the Shelby Cobra. Carroll Shelby actually built three cars, one for my dad, one for himself and one for Bill Cosby. Carroll put his own mark on the car in a big way by painting the exterior black and installing a full black interior. That car and the sound it made was amazing. My dad paid six thousand five hundred dollars for the car and sold it for ten thousand five hundred dollars just before I got my driver's license. He wanted to make sure I was never going to be able to drive that car! I think the latest Shelby Cobra that sold at Pebble Beach went for nearly fourteen million dollars, so I guess dad's car is worth somewhere between ten thousand five hundred and fourteen million dollars.

Our days with Frank Sinatra were so special. Our house [in Palm Springs] wasn't going to be ready in time so we stayed with Mr. Sinatra for a few weeks, and he was such a generous man. One morning we were all having breakfast. Mr. S had his head buried in the newspaper but then asked his personal assistant, I think her name was Bonnie, to come in. They had a brief discussion behind the paper. Mr. S then folded the paper and said, "Boys, I'll see you tonight for dinner. See ya, Kenneth." After Mr. S left I said, "Dad, what was he doing? I could hear him say something. What was he doing?" It turned out that Mr. S read a story about a local family that was destitute. He told his assistant to send them seven hundred and fifty thousand dollars anonymously. In those days, the early seventies, that was a lot of money, but that was just what he did. He was a very generous, understated guy, and he was very personal. He would come bearing gifts at Christmas, and my dad was very fortunate to know him. My dad was loyal, too, and that's why Mr. S trusted him. They had a great relationship and my dad took a lot away from that. Frank would always say, "Don't let your mouth spoil the moment." My dad was big on the silence as opposed to talking.

Growing up, I remember being on tour and traveling to certain events. One time at Firestone Country Club, Mike Souchak picked me up and threw me into the air. He was a great guy, winning around fifteen times during the fifties and sixties, but he didn't realize how low the ceiling was. My head blew straight through the paneling and made a real mess.

My mom would talk about how a lot of the guys would travel together and how Arnold Palmer would always leave his door open and I would run in, jump up and down on the bed and watch cartoons. Tony Lema would drive my dad's car to tournaments with my mom's brother, Bruce McClain, while my dad would fly in. It really was a special time to travel in those days. Arnold and Tony were very close and it was a real shock when Tony died in that plane crash.

I watched my dad win his last tournament, the Lucky International Open in San Francisco at Harding Park. It was fitting that he won his last tournament there as that was where he hit his very first golf ball. It was 1966, and he had just had surgery on his hands the previous summer. He was suffering from carpal tunnel syndrome, which was not recognized as such back then, but it was from hitting too many golf balls. His roommate at San Jose State was Bill Walsh, just before Bill became a famous football coach, and he told me, "Your dad would get up at five o'clock every morning and go out pounding golf balls until seven o'clock, hitting two hundred to three hundred balls before he'd go off to work at the sorority and other places." I guess it was just ingrained in him. The weather was particularly cool at that event and my grandfather had set up a pot of paraffin wax on a stove. At the turn, my dad put his hands into the wax to warm them up. He then returned to the tournament to finish the round.

Although he suffered back problems and other issues, his hands were by far the worst. We had a family friend out in Akron, Ohio, Dr. Walter Hoyt, who had served under General George Patton. Dr. Hoyt looked at my dad's hands and said, "Ken, you know, I think you've got a problem here." Previously, my dad had been treated at the Mayo Clinic where they cut his hand open and tried to straighten everything out, giving him cortisone injections to help with the pain. His left hand recovered but his right didn't, and at one point they thought he was going to lose his fingers or even have to have part of his hand amputated.

Dr. Hoyt decided to go back in and try to figure out what was going wrong. When he opened up the back of my dad's right hand he found that the scar tissue from the Mayo Clinic operation was growing over the tendons and restricting the blood flow. Dr. Hoyt went in with a scalpel and cleaned it up to a certain extent. Dad's hand did recover slightly but not to where it needed to be. He continued to have issues, but there came a point where he could no longer open his hands. When he lost his hands, he lost his game.

When we moved to the desert the warm weather was really good for dad and his circulation improved slightly, but when his golf career ended his broadcasting career started, and that was the best thing that could have happened to him. Tim, myself, and Peter and Andrew, my two boys, saw dad in action at the President's Cup in 2000. We saw him up in the booth, and he knew all the players' playing habits and what their talents were. It was simply amazing for us to realize his passion for golf and we really saw him reliving his tournament days with the opportunity that broadcasting offered him. My dad had the chance to work with some great guys, especially those who had some color behind them and an appreciation for the game, but still maintained a nice balance between entertainment and tradition. He started his broadcasting career with Vin Scully, Jack Whitaker, who was just a prince of a guy, Pat Summerall and then eventually worked with Jimmy Nantz. Thirty-five years and the longest running sports analyst in broadcast history. Not bad, eh?

One of my favorite memories of my dad is when he was aboard the USS John F. Kennedy, flying in and taking the controls of an F-14 Tomcat. The admiral was the guy who put my dad through all the training, making sure he was capable of handling the g-forces that these jets create. They had to give him a handle, a name, a call sign to put on his suit. Dad was regularly out on deck giving golf lessons and tips to all the guys on board, so his handle was TIPS. They embroidered that on his flight suit, and man, was that neat, especially when they gave him the suit to keep as a souvenir of the flight.

"I dropped my putter and I raised my arms up to the sky," Venturi told the Associated Press in 1997. "I said, 'My God, I've won the Open.' The applause was deafening. It was like thunder coming out there."

Venturi was so weak that he could not reach into the hole to get his ball, so Raymond Floyd, his playing partner, did it for him.

"I felt this hand on me, and it was Raymond Floyd handing me the ball," Venturi remembered. "I looked at him, and he had tears streaming down his face."

As Floyd later told the Associated Press, "He was running on fumes. If you had asked him his name, he could not have told you. It is one of the most heroic things I have ever seen."

Associated Press

When I was a teenager I was kinda into everything, playing football, basketball and baseball. I also made the swim team, but the one sport I enjoyed the most was boxing. That took up the entire winter, as we trained from October all the way through early April, and it meant that mostly I didn't have to be outside in our crappy, cold winter weather! I lived in a fringe county of Washington, D.C., which was and still is a very tough place with some hardened fighters, street fighters if you will. My dad got me involved in boxing and Boy's Clubs because I was so small, he knew I had to learn how to look after myself somehow. The various clubs were a great way to channel these fighters into an organization that would help them develop those skills that, you know, seemed to come so easily to them.

I grew up in the same county as a particularly talented individual. We fought at the same weight, and he belonged to the same club as me. Like everyone else, I always dodged having to spar with him. It was obvious this guy was special; he was super fast and his hand speed was incredible. He was absolutely fearless in the ring but he carried with him such charisma. He was articulate, fun and a total entertainer. In a way, I wish I had sparred with him because I'd have had a great story to tell, the day I got in the ring and got my ass kicked by Sugar Ray Leonard.

I was tiny at sixty-five pounds, but had to lose ten percent of my body weight, six pounds, to make my weight of fifty-nine pounds. For the guys who needed to lose weight it was a dangerous time. On one occasion there were six of us, and we'd go run five miles before the coach would pile all of us into a VW Beetle that he'd been warming up. We were still in our sweats, but he covered us with a plastic tarp and turned the heat on full blast. We'd sweat off that weight pretty quickly, and it could've killed us. The only saving grace was that once we made weight we could go and eat all we wanted. It didn't matter after the weigh in. I was always small, and at sixteen I was fighting at the welterweight level of one hundred forty-seven pounds, which is where Sugar Ray Leonard was for most of his professional fighting career.

We had a guy at our club by the name of Terry Butner who went to the final trials for the 1976 Olympics that were held in Montreal, Quebec. He ended up losing in his final round to the guy who actually went to the games and represented the U.S.A. in one of the best boxing teams that we have ever had. I was asked to be one of Terry's sparring partners, and at that time, was a little heavier at one hundred and sixty pounds as I hadn't been in the ring for a couple of years. I agreed and hopped into the ring. Just as I

was thinking about throwing my first punch, all of a sudden I was eating three punches to my face. This guy was so quick, and I really had to think "Why am I doing this?" I only sparred for a couple of months but I really did enjoy it.

Terry and I got along great. When we left the gym one night these three guys came up to us. One of them said, "You Terry Butner?" Terry replied, "Yup." The guy continued, "You the boxer?" Again, Terry just replied, "Yup." The guy carried on, "You a little guy." Terry again replied, "Yup." The guy then said, "I'm gonna kick your ass." Terry snapped back, "Nope." The guy was getting ready to square off when Terry just threw one punch and knocked him out cold. The other two just mumbled, "You bad. You bad," got their friend, and left. I'm so glad Terry took care of that. I really didn't want to get into a street fight with any of those guys.

When I was ten years old, I caddied for my dad one day and really fell for the game of golf. I grew up by the University of Maryland golf course and when I was twelve I started working there, helping with the range, the carts and general maintenance. I spent a lot of time working there or hanging with my buddies who played golf, and it was a natural progression for me to take up the sport. As I got older I attended the University of Maryland and tried out for their golf team. I didn't make it that year, missing out by one shot after twelve rounds of qualifying. I was a pretty good player coming out of high school but didn't have a good stretch in the final qualifying round, making a nine or ten on the second hole of the par three course that I grew up on. I hit it left off the tee and straight into a dry creek bed. I tried getting it out but it just got in worse shape and I ended up making a really big number that cost me my place on the team. I flunked out of school the first year and, not making the team, went down to junior college for two years. I played on the college team, which was very strong, making the nationals both years I was there. My game was a lot stronger when I eventually returned to the University of Maryland, and although I wasn't the top player, I was very close to it, making the team with relative ease.

In 1981, I went on the Mini Tour, but I just couldn't make enough money and eventually ended up broke. Although I had a good time, I learned a lot and realized that I didn't want to go down that route again, so I got a job with a temp agency, Manpower. I cleaned up a burntout warehouse for about a month, but during that time, my coach got promoted to assistant athletic director and offered me a coaching job. I almost snatched his hand off as I was twenty-four years old at the time and would have almost done it for free. I was making eighteen thousand a year as a head golf coach. I believe at the time, if not still, I held the record for being the youngest head golf coach of anyone in the NCAA.

Moving forward, I was always one of the shortest players on the regular tour, not just in stature but in driving distance. I soon learned that it was okay, you just can't be short and crooked! I was definitely in the bottom third on distance, but I was long enough to compete, especially on certain narrow courses or those with a high rough or an aggressive tree line, where accuracy was key. I really excelled at those venues. I started playing the longer courses well with the introduction of hybrid golf clubs, which I consider to be the best game improvement club invented for every golfer out there. I think they're more important than balls, wedges, or drivers and I consider them to be the best thing since sliced bread!

The highlight of my golf career happened shortly after playing the Rail Golf Course in Springfield, Illinois, with Jack Nicklaus in 1988. I knew I was going to be playing in Augusta that year so I asked Jack if I could play a practice round with him when we got there. He said, "Sure, why don't you join Arnie and I on Wednesday." I just about threw up but managed to reply, "Really? Arnie?" He replied, "Yeah, we're playing at eleven a.m." That day was phenomenal. I showed up at the range at about seventhirty a.m. for our eleven a.m. tee time! I was as nervous as heck on the front nine, hitting a snap hook on the first, a slice on the second and another hook on the third, which prompted Jack to stride over to me and ask, "What the hell is wrong with you?" I replied, "Look, I'm a little nervous here. I can handle one legend at a time pal, but I got two to deal with here!" Throughout the round I heard stories about themselves, their history, Augusta,

Bobby Jones and Ben Hogan. There were stories from Sam Snead to getting standing ovations from the ninth hole all the way to the eighteenth. I have to pinch myself when I recount these stories. They still give me goosies. It was an incredibly special day and I feel blessed that I had such an amazing opportunity to play with the two of them. It's still hard to believe. Although I was so nervous and shot a forty-five on the front nine, I did recover to shoot a thirty-two on the back. Arnie and I won the back nine on the eighteenth, winning five dollars from Jack that I've yet to collect!

Finally, I've got to tell this simply amazing story involving Tiger Woods. I was at Firestone one year, I believe it was around 2001, when Tiger was in just great form and the guy to beat. We were under a rain delay and a group of us were gathered around this big table when Tiger walked in and sat down to join us. This was a bit unusual as he doesn't usually enjoy being a part of a larger group like that. I've always given him a lot of crap, and he loves giving the needle back. He was getting into free-diving, so I looked over at him and said, "Hey, I heard you're really into that free-diving stuff." He looked back and replied, "Yeah, I shouldn't be here today, though, I almost killed myself once." With that, conversations stopped and everyone's hanging on the next words out of Tiger's mouth. You could almost hear the proverbial pin drop. He then started telling the story and admitted that he committed a couple of real diving no-no's. Apparently, he was in, I think, Belize, where the water is just crystal clear. So he sees this shipwreck lying on the seabed and decides that he's going to dive down, on his own, to have a look at it. He decides to just jump in, stating he's got to the point, with all that SEAL training and everything, that he can hold his breath for about four minutes.

He reaches the wreck and starts looking around for a way in when he finds an open hatch. He goes inside the wreck but misses the fact that his fins are stirring up the silt in the boat. It went black in there, and he starts to get disoriented and couldn't find his way out. His heart rate got out of control, and he said to himself, "I'm Tiger Woods and I'm going to die in this stupid wreck. I'd better get control of myself." He managed to calm himself down, lowering his heart rate as well as his emotions, and started feeling around for the open hatch that he entered the wreck through in the first place. He found it and started swimming toward the surface, breaking through right before running out of air. That was pretty stupid of him, but the fact that he opened up enough to tell that story to us was, in itself, amazing.

****

"The game of golf would lose a great deal if croquet mallets and billiard cues were allowed on the putting green."

Ernest Hemingway

****

Section 2:
The Europeans

CHAPTER

9

NICK
FALDO

A lot of people don't really know how I started in golf or where I come from. Initially, I was a carpet fitter, and I left school at age sixteen purely to become a golfer. I first started playing golf at fourteen years of age with my first round of golf. By fifteen I'd fallen in love with the game, and by sixteen I've left school. It was a pretty direct route and I had very trustworthy parents for which I will always be extremely grateful.

Back then I had a mate who ran his own one-manband carpet fitting business and, like those days we had back then, you know, a typical Wednesday when the snow is coming down sideways and you really can't go outside, I could give him a call at eight in the morning and say, "Hey, can I come and work for you today?" He'd let me go do some work for him and I got two pounds a day. That was my rate, the equivalent to about three bucks a day. It was a long time ago, mind you, and you could buy a house and a car for three bucks a day! That's what I did back then, mostly for a laugh, but I don't think I did that for more than a dozen times or so.

I definitely wasn't born with a silver spoon in my mouth. I worked my way up, played golf, eventually attended university in Houston, Texas, and made the PGA Tour from there. I became PGA champion after winning six majors, including three Masters and three [British] Opens, which I don't think was too shabby. Now all of a sudden I'm building golf courses, then I'm announcing, and now I'm putting golfing schools together. I kept asking myself, "What's next for Nick Faldo?" and I have to admit that I think there's still lots to come. When I look at what I've gone through, you know, I'm really quite proud of what I've achieved.

I was actually born in the back room of a Council house, [subsidized housing in the United Kingdom], and I asked my dad one day how much the rent was back when I was born. He told me you could get change from a dollar a week. How's that? Twelve and six, about eighty-five cents, was the weekly rent on the place. It was a nice house and I loved it there. It was my little world for the first eleven years of my life, and then we moved to the other side of town, I got into golf, and yeah, now I'm older, I have my television schedule set in stone. Outside of that, my Faldo Series is very important to me, and my golf design business is going well. I actually opened a golf course during our Grand Final at Mission Hills in China, and we have projects we are working on in Vietnam, Cambodia, New Zealand and China.

It's funny, because when I first came out on tour and, say, you were playing in a tournament in Asia, you'd have a different contract for that event with a Japanese golf bag, you'd be advertising Japanese clothing companies, and it was the same when Jack Nicklaus would come over to the [British] Open in the UK. He would be wearing Slazenger sweaters and have a Slazenger bag. Everybody would be changing their apparel for that country. Then suddenly the globe changed. Once global television happened people realized you can't do that, you can't be on the other side of the world, being on TV in America with an American contract, and be playing with totally different equipment. I guess that's what happened when the globe got smaller and, in a sense, everywhere you go, you're really on one stage as a golfer.

****

"The number of shots taken by an opponent who is out of sight is equal to the square root of the sum of the number of curses heard plus the number of swishes."

Michael Green,
The Art of Coarse Golf, 1975

****

Today, there are so many more opportunities in the golfing arena, not just the competition aspect, and it's an important message to get across to our young kids and students because only a very small percentage will ever make it as a top-level tournament player. Fortunately, now the golf industry has dozens of opportunities, whether it's course architecture, being a club professional, or working in the television booths and studios, there's so much more than simply playing the game. I'm very

63

fortunate in picking golf for my career as it seems that everyone outside the world of golf loves golf. I've met kings, queens and the Donald Trumps of the world—I designed and built two golf courses for Donald at Doral, Florida. I enjoy it when genuine people come up to me and say, "Wow, I've grown up watching you play golf since I was a kid." I'm very comfortable meeting people and talking with them about the game of golf because that's the common ground between you and them, and that's very, very cool.

On the topic of my Faldo Series, I have to tell you about the location in Casa Grande in Arizona. The project came to light after I was introduced to Casa Grande during a meeting with Michael Saunders and Ron Burke. I was asked about being involved in a project to help bring a golfing center to Casa Grande, so I quickly put my thinking cap on and introduced them to my Faldo Series, which had, at that time, forty events in thirty different countries, mainly Europe and Asia, reaching some seven thousand kids in some wonderful locations around the world. Interest in the series has grown considerably with social media and the likes of Twitter. Kids who are climbing mountains in Nepal can tweet to other kids who are playing golf in Cambodia.

We started the series in 1996, and about twelve or so years ago a young player named Rory McIlroy played on my series. I put a Team Faldo together that included the likes of Rory, and about ten years ago, with the success of the European Series, we decided to take the project to Asia. We were fortunate enough to have this young player introduce us to Asia, and she really helped us over there. Her name was Yani Tseng, and to have her involved in the series was perfect timing, as Rory had just won the Honda Classic to become the world number one men's player while Yani was the world number one women's player. Basically, we had two kids that came through the Faldo Series both become world number one players.

My goal with Casa Grande was to make it a practice course, to have different environments out there, with the bigger picture of offering students the opportunity to come there and educate themselves academically, as well as educate themselves as golfers.

I was brought this opportunity when I was really heading in a different direction. But from the very first meeting with Michael and Ron, and after touring the facility, we all agreed there was so much potential there that we just couldn't pass it up. It's going to be important for kids and students, but more so for parents, to know that it's going to be, what I would call it, a golfing boot camp right on their doorstep, on site. Academics will be taught alongside golf. We're giving them the chance to come to the party, if you will. All they have to bring are determination and work ethic.

Initially, and coming from the UK, the most important thing everyone was looking for was sunshine so you could work and practice at your game in a consistent manner. There's nothing to hold you up. We all fled to Florida initially, but we gradually realized exactly what Arizona had to offer. We're not just looking at local kids to fill the school, but we want kids from around the world to consider us here. In Europe we have kids from China and India, all sorts of places. They can't progress into the American series from their countries, so these schools give them a great option to further their golfing careers as well as their education through universities. I think the location in Casa Grande will be perfect for this purpose.

I was born in the small mining village of St. Martin's in Shropshire, England. My dad was a farmer. The nearest golf course to me, Llanymynech, was fourteen miles away and had fifteen holes located in Wales and the other three in England! I only used to get to play nine holes on Wednesday in the summer once I'd milked the cows, and on Sunday we used to milk the cows in the morning, go play golf, and then get back to milk them again in the evening. I really didn't have a lot of time to play in those days. It wasn't until I left there at age sixteen that I started to play golf a little more, and I saw my game improve vastly. I was pretty well selftaught until I received some coaching from John Jacobs, Bob Torrance and Peter Cowan, each having a different and positive impact on my game.

The great thing was that Sandy Lyle was also born in Shropshire, and we ended up as playing partners on the same team together, the Shropshire Colts. When we turned professional, although we were both born in England, I played for Wales while Sandy represented Scotland. He was probably one of the best players in the world at sixteen years of age, but people didn't realize just how good he was. Being around him really helped me step up the standard of my golf as I had to keep up with him, that's if I wanted to be a professional golfer. He was the best role model anyone could ever have, and my golf improved significantly because of that.

I started playing professionally in 1976. When I was on the European Tour in 1979, I would drive from tournament to tournament in my Volkswagen Caravanette. I traveled everywhere in that van and golf was a bit different in those days. You could go down to Portugal and play there one week and then the tour would move to Spain the next week, followed by France and Italy in quick succession, and you could drive from event to event. I didn't have much money in those days and baked beans were definitely a diet staple, cheap and cheerful, but it was such a great experience. You can't do that anymore as you might play Italy one week and then have to go to Dubai, which seems like halfway around the world. I'm really grateful for the impact golf has had on my life. I mean, in 1983, I was traveling around in my Volkswagen Caravanette, and ten years later I was flying in my own private jet! Quite a change, for sure.

****

"There is no similarity between between golf and putting; they are two different games, one played in the air, and the other on the ground."

Ben Hogan

****

I remember we used to go to Africa, Nigeria, Zambia, and Kenya and those were pretty frightening at times. I can't recall the number of times I've had a machine gun stuck in my face, but believe me, it's once too many. We would get caught up in the coups those countries were susceptible to and I remember in Nigeria, it was definitely "first come, first served" as all we wanted to do was get on the plane out of there. Most of the time it was the police who would stop our car, stick their guns in our faces, and demand, "Who are you? Where are you going?" Once I replied, "I'm going home. Where do you think I'm going?"

In 1983, I was picked to play at the PGA National Golf Club in Palm Beach, Florida, for the European Ryder Cup team. Tony Jacklin was the team captain and he wanted to make sure he had everything in place for the European players, meaning better clothing, golf bags, travel and accommodations. He wanted everything to be first class for his players, and those were the terms he needed or he wouldn't take the job. Everything was settled accordingly, and off we went to Palm Beach. I took Glendryth, my girlfriend at that time and my wife now, with me. Obviously, once we got there, we were committed to make appearances and attend certain events and parties for public relations purposes. One event in particular was a dinner at a restaurant at the local marina. Glendryth and I were standing with Sam Torrance and his wife in the hotel's bar/ reception area trying to figure out where we had to go when we saw Fuzzy Zoeller get in his car. We had these really nice white Cadillacs to drive and I looked at Sam and said, "There's Fuzzy, he must know where to go, we'll just follow him." It seemed like a good plan, but what we didn't realize is that we hadn't really read the full details of that night. We thought that the U.S. and European teams were having a joint event when in reality we were meant to be at two different locations. So we jumped in the Cadillac and start following Fuzzy.

We go through this gated area and it's really nice in there. We stop where Fuzzy stops, at a house just a little way into the neighborhood. Fuzzy parks his car, and we park ours, and then we see Jack Nicklaus standing by the front door of the house. We're thinking, "Wow, this is really nice, Jack's here to welcome us to his party. This is going to be great." So, we go into the house and Jack starts showing us around. He shows us the house, the gardens, and the grounds, and we are well impressed until Jack figures out what we've done and says, "Mmm, I don't think you guys are at the right place. I think you're meant to be at the marina which is about a mile over there." You could see the marina restaurant way over there, across this bridge, and that's where we were meant to be. The whole thing was just brilliant, Jack was there and he was so friendly, welcoming us into his house and showing us around. It was so funny, the evening we crashed Jack Nicklaus' house and he gave us a guided tour.

For my first match in that 1983 Ryder Cup, Tony Jacklin paired me with Sam Torrance, and we're playing against Ben Crenshaw and Calvin Peete. We practiced on the range and I can't explain how nervous I was. I told Sam as we reached the first tee box that I thought I was going to be sick. Sam turned to me and told me not to worry, he'd look after me. With that, Sam stood on the tee box with a three wood and proceeded to hit his ball straight out of bounds right. I get my one iron off the tee and down the fairway, made the green in two, and sunk the putt for birdie. On to the next hole and there's water all the way down the left, and sure enough, Sam put his tee shot in the water. I hit it down the middle, made a par, and halved the hole. When we came back the other way off the third tee box the water was on the left again and sure enough, Sam stepped up and blasted it straight into the water for a second time. I kept it on the grass and managed a birdie on three, so I went birdie, par, birdie, and the match is all square. After that, Sam woke up and made a few birdies but from what I was told, it's just another Ryder Cup rookie experience that seems to happen more often than not. You know, I'm thinking he's the more experienced player, and he's the one falling apart, not me.

In 1986, I was diagnosed with ankylosing spondylitis, which is basically an inflammation of the spine, and I've been on medications for it ever since. They really didn't know much about it back in those days, and when I was diagnosed with the issue the doctor said I could be fine or I could be in a wheelchair within ten years. Thanks, pal, I thought to myself, that was nice of you! I've done pretty well since the diagnosis and the pills I take definitely help me. I think my best year was 1987, which was when I started taking them. Things really turned around, and I won, I think, eight tournaments that year with winnings in excess of two million dollars.

As the term rain delay sinks in, it reminds me of the World Match Play Championship held at Wentworth, just outside of London in 1987. A big storm rolled through with hurricanes, I believe, on the south coast of England. Sunday's play was canceled and a thirty-six-hole final was played on Monday. I was playing Sandy Lyle in that final, and whoever came out the victor would be the first British champion in the history of that event. Two old schoolboys battling it out against each other over thirty-six holes, and I bloody beat him on the last hole. I should have known that's how it would turn out as in the rounds previous to the final I beat both Seve Ballesteros and Nick Faldo on the last hole. That's three great scalps for sure!

In the U.K. they have an award called Sportsman of the Year, hosted by the BBC. Well, they contacted me and asked if they could have my 1991 Masters trophy for the show. No results are ever given ahead of time, so I started thinking I could be in the running for something, after all, why else would they want my trophy? I agreed to ship it to them, so I packaged it up and sent it via Red Star delivery, usually a high-priority shipping method via train back then. They received my trophy and I attended the event, finishing third. Unfortunately, when they returned the trophy to me, via the same Red Star service, it went missing. I guess someone has a Masters trophy on their mantelpiece now or else it's in a rubbish dump somewhere. I never got the trophy back so I had another one made for me, I think by Garrards, the Crown Jeweler in London. The year I won the trophy was the last time it was made in the likeness of the clubhouse at Augusta as they changed its form after that.

I'm fortunate to have been to Buckingham Palace on two separate occasions. The first time I attended the Palace I received the MBE [Member of the Most Excellent Order of the British Empire] from Queen Elizabeth II, while my second visit was to receive the OBE [Officer of the Most Excellent Order of the British Empire] from Prince Charles. Basically, you get dressed up in your morning suit, top hat, tails and gloves, and go to Buckingham Palace. You do your bow and have a little chat before receiving your MBE or OBE. I have to say that I was really impressed with how much both Queen Elizabeth II and Price Charles knew about the game of golf as well as my accomplishments, and that really topped off two very special occasions. They are very nice awards, with the MBE given for winning the Masters in 1991 while the OBE was more for the Ryder Cup in 2006 at the K Club in County Kildare, Ireland, than anything else.

****

"Success in golf depends less on strength of body than upon strength of mind and character."

Arnold Palmer

****

I played with Nick Faldo in the Ryder Cup on two or three occasions, and we had a fantastic record together. We were probably two of the most unlikely individuals you would pair together but it worked so well because we were such completely different characters. Nick was great for me, and I think I was the same for him. He was so steady, he was just going to grind out for those pars, maybe make some birdies, and that just let me be myself, really aggressive, with a look at a birdie or eagle on every par five. It was a fantastic partnership.

Nick was a great partner in the Ryder Cup, but once that event was over, it was all bets off, he'd just blank you out. He was your best friend in team play but in regular singles-play tournaments, like the British Open, it was definitely you or him and he considered me, along with everyone else, his worst enemy. But that's just how competitive we all were back then.

I'm so honored and happy to be inducted into the World Golf Hall of Fame in September 2017. It really does change everything for me as I don't have to worry about getting invitations to other tournaments on the Champions Tour or make the top thirty-six in the Champions Tour rankings. It means I can play whenever I want to, and that eases a lot of pressure for me.

Becoming a professional golfer in Germany is a different process than in the United States. It's a step-bystep process. I was never a junior player. Basically, I was caddying so that I could actually afford to play golf, and I did that until I was fifteen. At that age I was old enough to become a PGA pro and I eventually joined the PGA Tour at eighteen. I was never an amateur, I never had a handicap, I simply went from caddy to pro.

I had very little experience and absolutely no tournament experience whatsoever. I played in my first tournament when I was fifteen or sixteen, but I was still only an assistant pro and tried to participate in the five or six tournaments that take place in Germany. Getting to play on the European Tour, with all the expenses involved, was going to be hard. I was trying to save as much money as I could from my job as an assistant pro and I lived very prudently. By chance there was this businessman from Cologne who saw me play in the National Semi-Pro Championship; I think it was in 1975. He watched me play and came up to me after the event was over and said, "Young man, if you ever want to play on tour, let me know. I'll help you financially." I replied, "Yes, I'd be interested." So we struck a deal where he would give me some money and I, in return, would give him about half of my winnings. It worked out great and took a lot of the pressure off me. It wasn't a whole lot of money, but it was enough to get me going, and it certainly supplemented my winnings. It was a deal that was based on my winnings, so if I didn't win he'd be out of pocket but if I did he would get fifty percent. He wouldn't lose a lot of money, but it gave me the security I needed to concentrate on my golf knowing, that if things didn't go well, neither of us would be out a bunch of money.

****

"Golf is a lot of walking, broken up by disappointment and bad arithmetic."

Author Unknown

****

You don't become a world-class golfer over the span of a year or two, and there was no other German golfer before me who was successful on tour that I could compare myself to. I knew I had to be patient, but I knew I wanted to try. When I was eighteen years old and still a teaching pro, I joined the Tour. I played on the European Tour and right away had a little success, finishing fifth in my third tournament, the Madrid Open. I constantly compared myself to the players out there and soon realized that my ball striking was as good as, if not better, than some of the other players. My short game was still lacking in places, so I figured out that if I worked on my putting and short game in general, I would be a match for those better players. Maybe I could even be one of the best. I just continually practiced that aspect of my game and slowly got better and better.

In 1979, I won the Under-25s Championship by seventeen strokes, a record that was in fact listed in the Guinness Book of World Records, and in 1981, I won the Money List. Over the years you get to know the colleagues you play with, day after day and week after week. They are constantly there. I was growing up and playing with the likes of Seve Ballesteros, Nick Faldo, Ian Woosnam, Sandy Lyle and Jose Maria Olazabal, some very lofty players, and I was beating them on a regular basis. Seve had already won several majors and I said to myself, "If Seve can win majors, and I can beat him in some of the events on the European Tour, why shouldn't I win a major as well?" It was a process that took a few years but, as my confidence in my short game improved, eventually it happened.

All right, so I'll jump straight to Augusta and the U.S. Masters in 1985. It's Sunday, the final round, and I'm playing with Seve Ballesteros. We were two shots behind the leader, Curtis Strange, who was playing with Raymond Floyd. I'll make a long story short here, I won the tournament, but it's what happened during that round that changed my life forever.

After the various presentations of the green jacket, both inside Butler's Cabin and on the eighteenth green for the spectators, I went back inside Butler's Cabin to where both the tournament and club presidents were standing. One of them asked me, "Why are there congratulations going on today? Were you watching the leaderboard at all today?" I looked at them and replied, "You know, I was trying not to watch the leaderboard too much because I learned that if I watched it all the time it would affect my game. If I'm in the lead I'll kind of try to protect that lead and I won't continue to play aggressively, which is what put me in the lead in the first place. I find that if I see my name on the leaderboard and I need to catch up to the leader I kind of get frustrated and down on myself, which is not good either."

So I really tried not to watch the leaderboard, but as I came off the ninth green, and I'm walking to the tenth tee, I took a quick glance over at the leaderboard, which was right there on the eighteenth green, and I literally said on live TV, which is broadcast to hundreds of countries and millions of viewers, "Jesus Christ, I can't believe I'm four shots behind Curtis Strange," because I thought I'd played really well. After seeing that my mindset was that I had to go for every flag and take every opportunity. Either I'm going to shoot a great back nine and win it or I'll finish tenth or twentieth! It doesn't matter, I want to win a major, I wasn't playing for second or third. Well, I was extremely aggressive and played lights-out golf, I think going five under on the back nine. I birdied five of the first eight holes and bogeyed the eighteenth, shooting a back nine of thirty-two, winning by two shots at the end.

On returning home following that win in 1985, I had hundreds of letters, mostly congratulatory letters, for me winning my first major, but a large number of them were from people saying, "Who are you to mention God's name in vain on national television?" I felt pretty bad about it but I wasn't a believer at that point of my life, however, it was a very powerful message nonetheless. Very soon after winning in 1985, Bobby Clampett invited me to his Bible study where I learned the meaning of God's word and progressed down the path of becoming a Christian.

Fast forward to 1993, when I won my second Masters. I was taken into Butler's Cabin again where the chairman said something like, "How does it feel to win the U.S. Masters twice? Was the first one better or the second one? Which stands out more?" I paused for a little, and then replied, "You know, it's awesome to win the U.S. Masters twice, maybe the greatest tournament in the world, but this one is really special for me because I won it on Easter Sunday, which is the day we celebrate the Resurrection of Jesus Christ." These are maybe the only two occasions that I've mentioned Jesus Christ on national television, in Butler's Cabin, in front of hundreds of millions of TV viewers. The first time was in a really bad way, but the second time was in a much more positive way.

Mark E. Squire

****

"Golf, like the measles, should be caught young, for, if postponed to riper years, the results may be serious."

P. G. Wodehouse
A Mixed Threesome, 1922

****

I'm happy to tell you that after some time away from the game, I'm playing a little bit of golf these days. In a moment of weakness, I entered the British Seniors event because it's back at Royal Lytham & St. Annes, where I won the Open Championship in 1969. I'm over there anyway for a month in August because I host an event called the British Par 3 Championship and I've got about a week to fill, and that was the British Seniors week, so I thought what the heck, I'm exempt anyway, I'll just enter. Believe me, my nerves are already beginning to get a bit twitchy over the thought of competing again.

The old nerves aren't what they used to be for sure, but I've just got through playing this morning in a little mini tour I put my name into called the West Florida Tour. We play two to three tournaments a week here in the Sarasota area. In order to get my head back in the game, I'm competing in a few of those events with these young bucks, and of course they hit the ball a good fifty yards past me every time. Nevertheless, it's getting me back into the competitive spirit.

I've lived through some good times, as well as some harsh times, during my years with the Ryder Cup. I played in seven Ryder Cups from 1967 through 1979, with the event in 1979 being the first European match. We weren't really competitive back then, and if you take a good look at it you'll see why. In America, you have about three hundred million people to choose from, where in Great Britain and Ireland we had about sixty million, which, combined with a climate that's not exactly conducive to golf, we had a bit of a handicap to start with.

Jack Nicklaus suggested that Europe be involved in the Ryder Cup in 1977, so in 1979 I basically played my last Ryder Cup, which, coincidentally, was the first European event. It was very one-sided through the 1960s and 1970s, but the watershed year came in 1969 at the Royal Birkdale Golf Club in Southport, England. We tied with the Americans after Jack Nicklaus conceded to me a twofoot putt on the final green, which later became known as "The Concession," to tie the match. This was a great gesture on his part and showed what an absolute gentleman of the game he was.

The form of the Ryder Cup was a little different in those days. I played two singles matches on the final day, with me playing Jack in the morning, nipping him four and three. Honestly, he wasn't in top form, but it was close all afternoon. It's interesting to note that 1969 was actually Jack Nicklaus' first Ryder Cup. The PGA in America had an eligibility rule that you had to be a member of the PGA for god knows how many years before you could be picked to play. Although Jack Nicklaus touted his demolition of the majors in 1962, his very first Ryder Cup did not take place until 1969.

In the 1980s, I took the helm of the European Ryder Cup team. Having played so much in America, I felt there was a lot left wanting when it came to organizing the European side of the event. Essentially, I felt that the American team had almost everything handed to them on a plate when they turned up to play. They had first-class transportation, the best in clothing and other apparel, and so on. Meanwhile, we were traveling in the back end of a bus wearing anything anyone would give us and basically, we were a couple of games down before we even turned up to play! The first things that got addressed when I took over were exactly those issues. I remember we traveled on the Concorde, just as the Americans had done previously, instead of on a bus. We upgraded our clothing and I created the team room, a place we had never had before, a place where players could gel instead of huddling together for two or three minutes in the corner of some locker room somewhere. Once we got these things organized, I felt that we were at least on a level playing field before the matches started.

Right at that point we were fortunate enough to have a large number of Europeans all getting into their top form at the same time. We got Seve Ballesteros on board, who at that time was arguably the best player in the world, followed by Nick Faldo, Sandy Lyle and Ian Woosnam. These guys, and more like them, had just come off winning majors. The confidence that we gained from a really good Ryder Cup in 1983 at Palm Beach Gardens, Florida, although we lost by a point, gave us the confidence to win the event on American soil for the first time in twenty-eight years in 1985 at Muirfield Village in Dublin, Ohio. That win kind of changed the Ryder Cup forever, and it's been very competitive ever since.

Seve Ballesteros was a member of the Ryder Cup team in 1983, but he was such a difficult person to pair up because he was such an intimidating guy. Even his team members were intimidated by him. He had so much charisma. Anyway, we had this young kid on the team, only twenty years old, named Paul Way. It was his first Ryder Cup so I paired him with Seve, and I wouldn't say Paul was arrogant, but he was pretty sure of himself and I felt comfortable with the pairing. I paired them up for the first foursome and four-ball match the first day and they either won or halved their matches. On the second day, I paired them again, and I thought all was well until one of the Spanish officials came over to me at lunchtime on the second day and said, "Well, I think you need to talk to Seve. He's not happy." So I said, "Okay, I'll go and find him." I find Seve, who's eating his lunch, and ask him what the problem was, why he wasn't happy, and he said to me with his Spanish accent, "This boy I play with, I have to hold his hand all the time. I have to tell him which club to play, how far pin is. I'm like his father." I replied, "Seve, you are his father." I pointed to his head and said, "Is that a problem?" He looked at me for a few seconds and then the penny dropped. He confidently said, "For me, no problem." They went off and beat Bob Gilder and Tom Watson in the afternoon, putting a lot of points on the board during that Ryder Cup and making it a very close match.

****

"Professional golf is the only sport where, if you win 20% of the time, you're the best."

Jack Nicklaus

****

I remember when I was younger playing with a kid named Christy O'Connor. He was unbelievable. In the mid sixties he was older than me, I think he's eighty-eight now, but I saw him a couple of years ago and he's still in great shape. He was a great player but you didn't see him play much over here in America. He would play some Ryder Cups and maybe some very special occasions, but in 1965, he did come to America and finished fifth in the Carling World Open at Pleasant Valley Golf Club in Sutton, Massachusetts, which, coincidentally, was my first visit to America.

I really enjoyed myself when I got my PGA Tour card and started playing events over here. I remember playing with Tom Weiskopf in the 1960s, and I butted heads with Lee Trevino on quite a few occasions. I came off worse most of the time! I got some vengeance in 1985 when we won the Ryder Cup and he was the losing captain. He was such a tremendous player in my mind, and I was trying to be as good as I could possibly be; it was a serious business.

I have to admit, like other players, I do have my embarrassing moments in my career that were focused on my putter for the most part. Later in my career, after I quit playing on the regular tour in 1982, I got the "screaming ab-dabs" with the putter. I was concentrating and knew that I had to follow through properly, but in Madrid, with a putt on the last hole of no more than a foot, I hit the ball twice before it went in the cup. Stuff like that, it was tension personified, and I was all out of whack for quite some time, putting like an idiot on a number of occasions. You feel like you're letting your fans down, you know. I had a lot of people following me back in those days, and I guess the pressure manifested itself as much in my putting than in any other part of my game. In order for me to move on from these issues and prepare myself for the Senior Open, I had to face up to them and try to understand what was going on. I figured out that I got into that state by being overgolfed, and I put myself under enormous pressure every time I played. Those memories are still in there, but if I can get myself into a more relaxed state of mind, understand that it's not life or death out there, and realize I've got enjoy it as much as I enjoyed it when I first picked up the game, I should be good.

I am a self-taught golfer and I was very determined, learning by watching as many good players as I could. I worked very hard, and when I came to America, I worked with Tom Weiskopf and others. I knew I was good but I couldn't control the speed of my swing, so I worked very hard in the 1960s with Tom Weiskopf. Tom, in turn, had worked with Tommy Bolt. Bolt had a wonderful swing, and I got to know him very well as he started teaching me the importance of the lower body in the swing. He also taught me how to control the speed of my swing with the lower body, letting my legs take the lead. I hit thousands and thousands of balls until it felt natural. Simply being able to play on tour full time with the likes of Jack Nicklaus, Arnold Palmer, Lee Trevino and all the other greats you start to realize that, if you're going to learn from them, you'd better learn quick!

Section 3:
The Americans cont. & South Africa

CHAPTER

13

LARRY
MIZE

When I was growing up in Augusta, I was the youngest of three children and no one in my family played golf. My dad started when he was about thirty-five years old and, being the athlete that he was, quickly became a one-handicap golfer. I would go to the course with him, and sometimes my mother would join him as she started to play a little too, but it was my father who had the biggest impact on me. I was the only one of the three kids who actually took to the game, and I guess it was inevitable that playing golf with him and growing up with the Masters literally right outside the back door, I would eventually make golf my career. It was fortunate that my dad had a membership at the Augusta Country Club. We lived alongside the ninth fairway, and if I looked over the backyard fence I could catch glimpses of the twelfth green and thirteenth tee at Amen Corner, watching the golfers as they played those holes. I was about nine or ten at the time and just starting to understand what the Masters and Augusta was really about.

I was able to go to the Masters as a spectator probably from 1967 to 1971, and then in 1973 and 1974 I worked on the scoreboard on the third hole. That was the neatest experience, witnessing this amazing event every April, and simply falling in love with the game at such an early age. I honestly can't remember ever wanting to do anything else. It became my dream, and I guess I was stubborn and determined enough to keep working at fulfilling that dream. Augusta is a wonderful country club with a great golf course and a junior program with lots of good players. It was the perfect place to learn to play golf.

I was very excited to be working on the scoreboard. I remember thinking, "This is great! I've got a free ticket to go out there, with a lunch ticket so I get a free lunch too, and I get to work on the scoreboard." I recall Jack Nicklaus winning in 1972 but then in 1973 I was on the scoreboard with the officials going back and forth as to whether they were going to play or not because of the heavy rain. We were all getting soaked, just sitting in the rain by the scoreboard, not knowing what was going to happen when play was eventually canceled for the day. They came back and finished the final round on Monday with Tommy Aaron winning by one stroke. Yes, we all got soaked that day, but it was just so neat to be a part of it, you did your part of making it such a special tournament. You know, we all did it, we all took a peak through the holes in the scoreboard when we changed out the numbers. We did it then and I still see the guys and gals doing it now, taking a quick peek at what is going on and checking out the action on the course.

Working on the scoreboard on the third hole was the best as when you work the second half of the day, once the leading groups come through three, you take the numbers down, put them back in the box, and tidy up. By that time the leaders were only on holes four or five, and you could watch them play for the rest of the day, sometimes catching them on the practice range once they'd finished their round. I'd go sit in the bleachers at the driving range and watch these guys just hitting ball after ball. I knew I was going to learn something.

The first time I came to the Masters as a player was in 1984. It was such an exciting week for me. It was raining on Monday and I tried to play a little bit, teeing off ten, but the weather was just too bad. I walked over to eighteen, played that one in, and I was done. I did get out there on Tuesday and Wednesday, but on the first tee I was so nervous and excited to be there, I duck hooked my drives into the trees both days, one day coming to rest among them while the other day the ball went clear through to the ninth fairway!

Thank goodness I got those out of my system by the time Thursday came around because, as nervous as I still was, I was a little better controlled and managed to hit a nice drive straight down the fairway. My first year there was simply unbelievable and I finished tied for eleventh, a result that got me back in 1985. I remember that as I played the third hole, I looked up at the scoreboard and thought to myself, "Wow, I used to work on that scoreboard, but now I'm out here playing!"

✶✶✶✶✶✶✶✶✶✶✶✶✶✶

"Golf appeals to the idiot in us, and just how childlike golf players become is proven by their frequent inability to count past five."

John Updike

✶✶✶✶✶✶✶✶✶✶

Obviously, the most memorable moment in my entire golf career was defeating Greg Norman and Seve Ballesteros in a sudden-death playoff to win the 1987 Masters. It was an unbelievable time in my life, and my wife likes to reminisce about how I came to wear that purple shirt that day. This company, Aureus, that supplied my shirts, would send me stuff that was due to be released, so when I wore their shirts it was as if I was advertising the apparel they would be releasing fairly soon. When it came to picking out my clothes for that final Sunday, we were all staying in a room together at my parent's house. We had just put our son, who was just under a year old, down for the night, and the lights had been turned off. I had already picked out the black pants I was going to wear. I just needed a shirt. We went into the room and, since we didn't want to turn on the lights and wake up our son, we started feeling around for a shirt in the dark. When we woke up the next morning we discovered we'd picked a shirt with navy blue in it, which certainly wouldn't go with the black pants. We ended up with my selection, the predominantly purple shirt that would at least go with my black pants.

I've never worn that shirt again, but I do still have it. It's in a bag or a box in my closet. I've sent out replica shirts as they were in demand for quite some time, but I still have the actual shirt from that day. However, there was this event I was playing in, the World Series of Golf, in Akron, Ohio, later that year. I'd played really well on the first day and was tied for the lead. I got up that Friday morning and decided I was going to wear that shirt again until Bonnie, my wife, turned to me and said, "No, no, no. You can't do that! Don't wear that shirt again. They'll butcher you if you wear that shirt. You know they'll give you a hard time." So I didn't. I've never worn that shirt again, but my kids have worn it for dress-up day at school. They have this Decade Day, and two of my boys have each worn that shirt on their particular day. It was so funny. They had the black pants to go with it and really looked the part. It was totally their call too. They just got to thinking about it, and it's what they chose. I had no problem with it, didn't even offer a suggestion. I just let them get on with it. It was probably the early 2000s at the time, and most kids there didn't even see the correlation. Some of the teachers did because they remembered my win, but not the kids.

Looking back to that day and that tournament, it's still so unbelievable for me. I know I overuse that word, but it was my childhood dream come true. There's no tournament I'd rather win than the Masters; it's the ultimate for me. It's been a tremendous blessing for me and my family, and I'll never take it for granted. The day Jack Nicklaus, my childhood idol, placed that green jacket on me in Butler Cabin couldn't have been more perfect. "Well done. Good job," were the words that came from his mouth that day, and having him shake my hand after he put the jacket on was so special. I have a picture of that on my desk in my office and I'll treasure it forever.

When I think about my career, I realize how fortunate I was to play in the company of the world's top golfers, but I always smile when I think of Lee Trevino. He just loves to talk and entertain, he's so funny. We were playing in a tournament in Paris, France, and the greens were a little rough. The ball would bobble and bounce its way toward the hole. You never knew, even if you'd chosen the correct line, whether it would take a detour! Anyway, Lee makes a putt on this hole, and his ball is bouncing all over the place. He turns to me and says, "Hey, did you see my ball on that last putt? It was bouncing so much I thought Charles Barkley was going to come along and dribble off with it!" There are other comedians on the courses out there, but that line from Lee was just perfect. It summed up the course for sure. He just made it more entertaining.

Every year on a Tuesday night at the Masters, there's a dinner for past Masters champions. Back some time, in the mid to early nineties, I was making my way out after the dinner. Everybody was hanging their jackets back in their lockers and getting ready to leave when I noticed that Gene Sarazen didn't have a ride back to his hotel. It was perfect timing. I said to him, "I'm going to be driving past your hotel. I'll give you a ride." I got to talk with a golf legend about golf and his life, and I'm sure I tried to hit every red light that night. It was a pure coincidence, but to have oneon-one time with him was very special. It was a real thrill for me.

CHAPTER

14

ARNOLD PALMER

"Arnold transcended the game of golf. He was more than a golfer or even great golfer. He was an icon. He was a legend. Arnold was someone who was a pioneer in his sport. He took the game from one level to a higher level, virtually by himself."

Jack Nicklaus—AP Sept. 2016

Playing golf during my early years was filled with thrills that I recount on a daily basis, and some still give me goosebumps. I distinctly remember playing my first round in the Masters in April 1955 with Gene Sarazen. He was such a big name, and I'd already read his books and knew a little about him. I knew he played at a fast pace, but as I got to know him, I began to understand what a really great guy and gentleman he was and I will treasure these memories for the rest of my life. To play with him in my first round at my first Masters tournament was quite the thrill.

I'm so fortunate to live the life I have. I sometimes stop and just think, "Wow, did I really get to do that?" I got to know Walter Hagen well, and it was hard to see him when he became ill and wasn't doing so well. He became a very good friend of mine, and when I won the British Open at Royal Birkdale in 1961, the first congratulatory phone call I received was from Walter. That meant so much to me. Getting to know all those guys gave me a bigger respect for the game of golf and the people, such as Walter Hagen and Gene Sarazen, who helped make the game what it is today. I could go on and on about my time playing golf with Sam Snead, and Byron Nelson was one of my real heroes. All of these golfers were such wonderful individuals who, as I said, helped make the game of golf what it is today.

With sixty-two PGA Tour titles including seven majors under my belt, I always felt I missed out by never winning the PGA Championship. I'm sure many of you will remember that 1968 PGA Championship in San Antonio, Texas, when I made a couple of great shots on the last hole, but then missed a ten-foot putt that would have sealed the championship for me. As it was, Julius Boros got up and down from seventy yards away in the fairway to take the title that year.

Those things you always remember, like the Masters at Augusta in 1961, where I had a one-shot lead going into the last hole that would have won me that tournament for the second year in a row. I let my mind get away from me for an instant and put the ball in a trap, ending up shooting a six on that hole and finishing second. There are lots of "what if" moments in my career; I could recount events at the Olympic Club in California, Brookline in Massachusetts, and Oakmont in Pennsylvania. I could talk about these for hours.

Bringing these events to mind also brings back quite a few embarrassing moments in my golf career, the majority of which I won't talk about because I really don't want to remember them quite that well. However, when I heard that Jack [Nicklaus] recounted a story where he shanked a shot off the twelfth tee at the Masters in Augusta, narrowly missing Bobby Jones, I guess I can share this gem. I remember playing at Greensboro, North Carolina, one year. I had a real chance to win the tournament when I came across this really narrow bridge made from railroad tracks or ties, something like that. I decided I was going to cross it and got about halfway across when I lost my balance and fell in the creek. There are some shots that I wish I had made better choices about before hitting, but the way I saw it, I was putting these experiences into a learning curve, and I used that knowledge to help me better judge similar situations that arose in future tournaments. I'm just happy that things like Twitter weren't around to cover those embarrassing moments back then!

Moving on to my tournament at Bay Hill in Orlando, Florida, one very substantial individual always comes to mind, and that was Payne Stewart. I got to know him very well; he was a Bay Hill boy. He used to come up to my office at the club when he was playing regularly and he would sit and pick my brain, ask me all sorts of questions. It got to the point where I really enjoyed listening to his questions and I tried to fill in the answers for him. I think he was a great player and did very well. However, on one occasion he did something that wasn't so colorful. Payne had a mind of his own. One day we had something going on at the club and he walked in but he didn't take his hat off. I said that he had to remove his hat. He actually got mad at me for making this request and he got up and went home. Of course, we got over that in time, but that was one of my pet peeves and he was mad at me for asking him to take his hat off. It seems quite funny as I tell it now but we were both big enough to not let it get between us, talking it over like the adults we were and making up for whatever differences we had.

When I think about my grandson, Sam, I actually wish he would come and pick my brain like Payne used to, and I have to say that if he walked into the club wearing a hat I'd get up and knock it off his head! Sam's a great guy and we're going through some rough spots in his game at the moment. We're trying to get him straightened out as far as thinking about the game of golf because, although he has a great personality, he worries way too much. We're helping him get over the little things that seem to bother him so much and that have a negative effect on his golf game.

Jack [Nicklaus] likes to keep in touch, but I know that he doesn't have the love for the game he once had. He much prefers tennis these days. I must admit I don't play as much as I once did, and I can understand Jack's thinking on the topic. It's tough when you can't play the way you played all your life. It becomes a difficult situation and I play most of my golf today in private. I don't play in public anymore except that Jack and I are going to play a little exhibition here in the desert in a week or so. I'm scared to death, and I'm sure he's really thinking about it too, but we're going to raise some funds for a really good cause. It's a tough one because you know that people remember the way you used to hit a golf ball when you were doing really well. Now you can't do all these things, and that makes it really difficult.

Mark E. Squire

"What other people find in poetry or art museums, I find in the flight of a good drive."

Arnold Palmer

Back in 1975, I was in Scotland the week prior to the British Open, to be played at Carnoustie Golf Links. Jack Nicklaus and I were playing a practice round at Carnoustie, just minding our own business, preparing for the following week's tournament. A lot of people take this opportunity to play for a little money, but Jack just wasn't into that. It isn't what he's interested in. He was out there to learn the golf course.

Two guys joined us on the second hole, which is a long par four. One of them was a guy named John O'Leary, a pro from Dublin, Ireland, while the other was Jack Newton from Cessnock, New South Wales, Australia. They wanted to play us, but I don't think Jack was in the mood as he said, "Well, I don't think I'm even going to play eighteen." We all played the second hole, and with about a hundred people watching us, Newton hit a beautiful three wood from the fairway, sticking it to within two feet of the pin, and that's a tough hole. We move on to the third, and Newton is playing to the crowd, shouting to the gallery, "Can you imagine, here we have two superstars among us that don't want to play the current European four-ball champions!" The crowd starts snickering, throwing out a few comments, and Jack is getting a little ticked with our playing partners.

Moving to the third hole, it's a short downhill par four with a berm that runs in front of the green, which forced us all to lay up. Nicklaus hit a really nice shot to about eight feet from the pin while Newton again sticks it in close, literally a kick-in birdie opportunity. Newton, again playing to the crowd, said to Jack, "You know, it's too bad we're not playing [for money], you'd be two down now." I wasn't on the green, so I was no help. Nicklaus came over to me, not having putt his ball yet, and asked, "Who is this guy?" I knew Jack Newton because I'd played practice rounds with him previously, so I said, "He's a good guy, he's just a little bit of that typical brash Australian, you know." Jack grabbed me, looked me straight in the eye, and said, "You play your ass off today."

He looked across to Newton and said, "Consider us one down if that's what you want to do. We will play, but I haven't putted yet!" He was challenging Newton's assumption that we're going to be two down after that hole and that Jack would miss his putt. Jack got up there, knocked it straight in and, glaring across to Newton, said, "Okay, we're one down, what do you wanna play for?" Newton responded, "Make it easy on yourself, big boys!" Nicklaus thought about it and said, "Well, I'll tell you what we'll do, we'll play automatic one down." This meant that, basically, every time someone lost a hole a new bet started, and our agreed rate was for twenty pounds a bet. The match was on!

By the time we get to the eighth hole, we had won every hole apart from the third, which we tied, and Newton and O'Leary were on their heels. Now the eighth is a par three, and the wind was blowing pretty hard. Nicklaus played a beautiful six iron, drawing it in against the wind. It looked great until the wind just plain knocked it down. You could see it land, skid across the green, and come to rest about twenty-five feet to the right of the hole. I remember thinking to myself, "What the heck do you have to do to get close on this hole?" I see these two guys a good fifteen to twenty feet to the left of the hole, at the back left corner of the green, sitting on their shooting sticks, and I think to myself that that might be a good line to follow. I hit the same six iron as Nicklaus and, trying to draw it a little, actually pulled it slightly to the left. It went high and left, but neither of us saw it land as the bunkers hide that part of the green. As we were walking up to the green we notice that both Newton and O'Leary missed the green to the right, but there was only one ball on the green. I was walking up the left side of the green while Nicklaus was busy signing autographs over by the gallery on the right. Newton and O'Leary were to the right of the green.

These two guys sitting on their sticks were almost comical. They were both about my age today, about seventy, dressed in plus-fours, plain shirts and ties, and wearing sport coats. They looked like they've just returned from a driven-bird shoot! Everything about them, their clothes, their little hats, they're just two buddies sitting out there enjoying the day. I walked across the green, and these two guys didn't say a word. Silent. I was looking for my ball when Nicklaus joined me on the green and looked in the hole. "Tom," Nicklaus shouted, "Your ball's in the hole!" Really, these guys showed no emotion. They never even clapped for a hole in one! Nothing to indicate that my tee shot might be something special. They were indeed statuesque! I turned to them and said, "Gentlemen, did you see my ball go in the hole?" One of them replied, in a fine Scottish brogue, "Aye laddie, we did." I exclaimed, "That was a hole in one!" The second gentleman pulled the pipe out of his mouth and responded, "Aye laddie, but isn't it only practice?"

Jack and I had birdied every hole but eight and twelve, with me making a hole in one on eight and Nicklaus making an eagle on the eighteenth. The third hole was tied. At the end of the round we stood on the eighteenth green and Nicklaus said, "Boys, what time does the eagle fly?" When you have cumulative bets like that, twenty pounds a bet, it makes a pretty tidy sum by the end of the round. Newton replied, "Well, I don't have that kind of money on me," to which Jack replied, "Well, in our country, fast pay makes fast friends. You don't make bets if you don't have the money to cover it if you lose." They were highly embarrassed, but Nicklaus said, "I'll tell you what, Tom, they can take us to dinner tonight and we'll call it square." I agreed.

What's ironic is that Jack Newton bogeyed the last three holes of the British Open the following week, putting him in a playoff with Tom Watson, which he lost, to give Tom his first British Open Championship.

Following this match, Jack Newton later commented to the Australian press, "I always loved Jack Nicklaus. I once won good money off my good mate Tom Weiskopf in Melbourne, and he always wanted to get me back. Finally he turned up with Jack as his partner, and he got me. I remember pressing and doubling and all sorts of things and losing the lot. Then when we finished I offered to pay Nicklaus and he said, "I will settle for a beer and a sandwich." I said "beautiful." Weiskopf never got any money. He wasn't happy."

Newton continued, "I was fond of Jack because I was one of those guys who wanted to learn and found him very approachable. I would go up to him and say, 'Any chance of a practice round?' and he would name a day and time. No drama. Some of the Yanks were reluctant to do that."

Eight years later, at the height of his career, Newton almost lost his life when he walked into a plane propeller. Despite the loss of his right arm and eye and severe abdominal injuries, he fought his way back to normal life and to golf, becoming a twelve handicapper while playing with one arm. He also became an exceptional commentator and fundraiser through his celebrity event.

****

Instead, they encourage the player to play well and become more open
"My courses do not intimidate.
to the enjoyable aspects of the game."

Tom Weiskopf

****

****

"The first time I played the Masters, I was so nervous I drank a bottle of rum before I teed off. I shot the happiest eighty-three of my life."

Chi Chi Rodriguez

****

It's 2002, maybe 2003, and I'm playing in a senior tournament, the Long Island Classic, with John Jacobs. Well, John's stories are legendary, and he's known for all the nonsense he gets up to, just ask Nicklaus or Trevino. So, we're playing this event and we're under a rain delay, sitting in the locker room, just jacking around and doing nothing in particular. John is conspicuous by his absence, but I know exactly where to find him. During every rain delay he goes out to his Cadillac, puts the seat down, stretches out, turns up the music, and lights up a cigar. He must go through about twelve to fifteen every day. I know he's in there because all I can see is smoke.

I fight my way into his car and ask him how long he thinks the rain delay is going to last. He says, "I dunno. Do you want to go with me? I have to go place a couple of bets at the local OTB." I said, "John, we're in a rain delay. We could start at any time." He peers outside at the rain and says, "No. No, no, no. They have my number, they'll call when they're getting ready to go." I gave in. "We won't be long," he says, "ten or fifteen minutes max."

We go about four or five miles to this betting place that he frequents every time he's in town, along with every other derelict in the world from Long Island, of which there are surprisingly many. We go inside, and I'm just hanging around while he's up there, sitting at one of the counters, putting down bets on all of the horse races coming up. I'm sitting there, trying to mind my own business, and not make eye contact with anyone. It's the sleaziest place of all time! After he finishes putting down all his bets, he saunters over and we leave. I said, "Have you had a phone call yet? Are we ready to go?" He replied, "Nope. They'll call when they're ready to go. We're not quite there yet. Are you hungry?" I exclaimed, "John, we haven't got time to go and eat. We've got to get back and warm up!" He told me not to worry, we'd get a call when it was time. I'm starting to get a little jumpy right about now but agree to go get some food, just so long as it's quick.

We drive to a pizza place about a mile down the street, get ourselves a couple of slices of pizza and wash them down with, of course, a few beers. We get done with that, and John then tells me that we've got to, "go down and get some cigars for his boy." I assume it's for a tour official. I'm a mess right about now as I'm supposed to be on the fourteenth hole and John on the ninth. We go get the cigars and he's got like about thirty of them.

As we start back toward the car, unfortunately John spots a group of these rag-tag guys. There were three or four of them, sitting on these wooden boxes, on the sidewalk in this old strip mall. One of them shouts across the road, "Hey guys, do you want some movies? We're selling movies over here." John goes, "Oh, we gotta go check this out!" I shouted, "No, John. We've got to get going!" I'm almost pulling my hair out in desperation but John doesn't hear me. He walks straight over and asks them what they've got. They replied, "We've got these movies for sale. We get them bootlegged!" John hands me this movie and said, "Here Gary, you'll like this one." John's pulling out all these movies, and they're strewn across the sidewalk when suddenly his phone rings. He says, "Butch just called. We're getting ready to start in fifteen minutes!" Let me remind you that we're still a good ten minutes from the course, on a good day! I plead to John, "Come on John, we gotta go!" He calmly says, "Hang on," and gives the guy some money for the movies. I think they were ten dollars a piece. I'll never forget it, this guy shot them through a hole in his jacket! He had a hole in his jacket and he goes to the movies and records them with his camcorder!

****

"They throw their clubs backwards, and that's wrong.
You should always throw a club ahead
of you so that you don't have to walk any extra distance
to get it."

Tommy Bolt about the tempers of modern players.

****

We get back to the car, and just as we start back toward the golf course, we spot these two squad cars. They pull us over, get us out of our car, and throw us up against the wall. John called Butch and said, "Uhh, Butch, we have a little problem here." I hear Butch say, "Come on John, just get back over here," John explains, "We're sitting here at the corner of whatever and wherever, in a strip mall, and we've been detained by the police." All I hear then is this scream coming from John's phone, "WHAT!!" John tells Butch, "You know, it's a long story, but don't worry, I've got your cigars!" We ask the cops how long we're going to be, and they explain they have to question us about the movies we bought. John goes, "Well, can you hurry it up? We're playing in a golf tournament, a senior tournament, the Long Island Classic just down the road." Then he gets on the phone to Butch. "Can you slow the proceedings down a little bit? Don't allow the guys to tee off until we're back in the parking lot!"

So, we sit there and get questioned by these cops about what these guys did, how they did it, and how they got us to buy the movies. The police eventually realized we had nothing to do with these guys and let us go. We were there for what seemed like an eternity. John and I got back in the car and drove about a hundred miles an hour back to the tournament.

As we pull in, John's on the phone to Butch. "Okay, release them now. We're getting in our cart and going out to the hole." I sure hope John gave Butch his cigars.

I was born in Joplin, Missouri, but grew up in Baxter Springs, a small town in southeast Kansas. I was very young when I started playing golf and the only golf facility there was a sand green municipal course. My father was an amateur, but I don't really know how good he was because he didn't have a handicap. They didn't have them back then. I lived in what could be termed baseball country as the great Mickey Mantle of the New York Yankees was born in the very small town of Spavinaw, Oklahoma, just across our state line. Baxter Springs was just on the Kansas side from where he grew up and, with only ten miles separating the two towns, all the kids played baseball. Everything was sandlot.

I found that I really enjoyed playing golf as it was something I could go off and do on my own. I didn't need a teammate like basketball or football. My father would take me out occasionally to play golf, but this town was small enough that every parent knew where every kid lived and who they belonged to. It was a very safe community and it wasn't a problem being on my own out there. My mother would take me to this little course and I'd play a couple of holes and then go look in the woods for golf balls, often coming back with poison ivy all over me, but it was something that I could go off and do on my own. I think that's what I found so intriguing about the game. I wasn't really sure how good I was as there was no one to compare myself to. Everyone else was playing baseball.

When I was fourteen we moved from that small town to Boulder, Colorado, leaving all my friends and memories behind me. It was saddening but the moment I got up there I found out my uncle sponsored a baseball team made up of fourteen- and fifteen-year-olds. My first day there I was on that team, so I was reasonably content.

We were staying in a room at this efficiency motel with its own kitchenette and dining area, right across the street from the municipal golf course, until our home was finished. My brother and I quickly realized that what was our plum in a small town became a harder walnut when you got to a bigger town. We would go across the street to the golf course and sneak in and fish golf balls out of the lake there, often getting chased off by the staff or other golfers. My mother entered me into a JC Golf Tournament for juniors and I was really excited because it was my first ever tournament. You can only imagine what I felt like when I managed to win that event. I think it was only two or three rounds but I still managed to win it. It didn't deter me from continuing on with other sports, playing basketball and football at high school, but it was at golf that I won the State Championship.

I didn't know what I wanted to be as a collegiate but I was good enough at football to get a full ride. There was certainly no one knocking on the golf door. I would have liked to go the golf route but my parents weren't wealthy enough by any means, so I followed the path of football. While that was difficult, I explained to people that it's the way I worked through college. I attended the University of Colorado where I was a two-time All-Big Eight defensive back as well as an academic All-American in football, but that didn't mean I was going to make it into the NFL. Each year my golf got better and I started winning State Championships.

I never had a coach in my life, but that's not to say that it was good or bad, that's just the way it was. There wasn't anyone to start coaching me even if I could have afforded it. My dad's motto was, "Don't start something you can't finish," and that's how I've basically led my life. It was great advice. I worked for my dad and uncle in construction as a laborer in the summers which meant I didn't have the opportunity to play in a lot of tournaments, so when I did get well into my college years and neared graduation I had a big decision to make for my marketing major—did I want to get into the business world or did I want to pursue football or golf? I also had to consider that it was during the Vietnam era and there was always the chance that a service commitment could be out there. I obviously chose golf, managing to win the individual NCAA Division I Championship in golf in my senior year out of Colorado, playing against some of the best players in the country. I proved to myself that even with the little amount of playing time that I had, I could compete on the bigger stage.

My talents were raw, I knew that, but could they get better? I didn't know the answer to that question, but I felt in my heart that that was the route I wanted to go. Once I made that commitment it was down to Florida in the spring of 1968, where I qualified for the PGA National, got my player's card and started on the PGA Tour that May. What I did and how I did it was unlike any of today's or yesterday's players. I did something completely different in my formative years, which I believe, added to my eventual success.

If a tournament I was playing in at any particular time became the subject of a rain delay, I was never one to simply hang around the locker room. I didn't want to get sidetracked by what anyone else was doing or what they were saying, good or bad. I didn't want to hear stories. I've been around enough locker rooms in my life that I didn't mind the peace and quiet, I really quite liked that.

I'm jumping forward to the Senior Championship that I'm playing now, and I had just come off of back issues the year before that caused me to withdraw from the Senior U.S. Open after seven holes. I wasn't playing much from June that year through the next year as I was still having back pain and spasms. I'd gone through injections in my back but I could tell that the issue was muscular. I was certain of it and I just had to let it heal. In the meantime my golf wasn't exactly sharp because of the time I was having to take off.

When I did start playing again I remember being at Valhalla where we had a great deal of rain. There's a stream that runs through the course, and with heavy rains it's quick to flood but the waters recede almost as quickly. It had rained quite heavily so this creek flooded quite a bit around the second hole and around the first green. When the rain stopped they had to let the creek subside. Then it would start raining again and the creek would flood the ninth fairway. It rained heavily on another occasion and the first green became an island while the ninth tee turned into a lake. We were going through these spats of rain and the water would rise and then subside only to rise again with the next rains that came. We had a rain delay during the final round and it appeared as if they were going to call play off for the day. They eventually decided to cancel play and the last round took place on Monday.

During one of the delays, while the locker room was nice, I'd been in there too much. So I'd get the weather report, grab my book and go to my car and read. The good thing is that doing what I did got me out of the dreariness of the banter between players saying whether we should just cancel the day and get out of there or wait it out. I didn't want to hear that negativity while I was trying to make a return from my back issue, with my game being tentative at best. I couldn't listen to it. I spent my time in the solace of my car, reading my book, which got my mind off of the banter that was going on. I could be with my thoughts and not get interfered with, finding that to be the best therapy. I was playing well in my comeback and had a real chance to win a major championship here. After all this stopping and starting I needed to perform well. I couldn't get caught up in this negative banter.

When play resumed on Monday I found myself in great shape and managed a win, and looking back upon that event, I think I won because I didn't hang around and get caught up in the locker room antics. I went to where I couldn't hear what was going on, making only the occasional trip in to check the status of play before, once again, retiring to the solitude of my car. For me, I was able to keep in contact with reality by disassociating myself from it.

A lot of rain delays are filled with negativity. Of course, there are a lot of funny stories that go around but you mostly sink to the lowest common denominator. Me, I decided I needed the space to focus on things that were good. I was on a fine line and I think that win really boosted my game going forward. I can remember thinking that I'd hurt my back and had been out of sorts for a year but now I'm finally back.

****

"Golf is an ineffectual attempt to put an elusive ball into an obscure hole with implements illadapted to the purpose."

Woodrow Wilson

****

I've played with Jack [Nicklaus] and Arnold [Palmer] for many years, but I don't believe in idols, I simply have a tremendous respect for anyone who plays the game. I don't try to throw stones at anyone because I know exactly what it takes to get there. It's up to each player to do with it what they can. Everyone can hit a golf ball, that's not the issue, it's what you do with it once it's there. How do you separate yourself from the pack? Participate in locker room activities over a rain delay or isolate yourself and take a nap? Do you go to your car and read a book? What do you do to keep yourself in the game, in the mindset, and not fall backwards? The best players who've ever played the game maintain a decorum. Across the pond, Faldo and Jacklin, the ones in my career that distinguished themselves, they all had a presence about them all the time whether it was raining or not. That's what I tried to learn from them.

They didn't hang around. I don't know what they did. Maybe they did and I didn't see them, I just tried to maintain a focus. When I stopped it was hard for me to get started again. It was hard for me to pick up and go. When there was a break in my train of thought my game was cerebral. I stayed in the game and kept it sharp. Anytime there was a lull in the action I had to keep my mental game in order. In some way, I think that's what Jack [Nicklaus] and all the great players did, they found a way to keep themselves in the game.

In trying to find my quiet corner of the world I found something that works for me. Some prefer the loud banter and company of others, which is absolutely fine, I have no problem with it. It just doesn't work for me.

Mark E. Squire

****

"Drugs are very much a part of professional sports today, but when you think about it, golf is the only sport where the players aren't penalized for being on grass."

Bob Hope

****

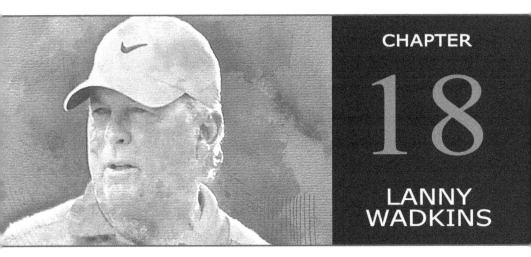

I was born in Richmond, Virginia, my dad drove a truck for a living while my mom taught school, barely making thirty thousand dollars a year between them. I attended Meadowbrook High School and then went to Wake Forest University on an Arnold Palmer golf scholarship.

I got married pretty young, which probably wasn't the smartest move, but Penelope and I were both young and it just seemed right. When I went through Q school [qualifying school] I was married, my wife was pregnant, and I was A-1 on the draft list, just about to be drafted to go to Vietnam. Then they had the draft slowdown and didn't draft anybody for the first three months of 1972, so I was able to go out and play golf. I was reclassified to H-1 and with my number being fifty-six, I was basically sitting on go, but that's how things were back then.

I'd had enough success as an amateur, finishing second to Bob Goalby in the 1970 Heritage Classic as well as ending up tied thirteenth in the 1971 U.S. Open, held at Merion [in Ardmore, Pennsylvania]. That result turned out to be huge as when I turned professional later in the year I had an automatic entry to the Masters in my rookie year, which was almost unheard of at the time. I knew the quality of the golfers out there, and I knew I could compete. I'd won at every level growing up so the PGA Tour, to me, was just another one of those levels.

When I was growing up I always looked up to Sam Snead. Sam was my idol, and he was a Virginia guy. Sam was who I pulled for all the time, and one of the great things about golf is that you get to play with your idols. I got to play with Arnold Palmer for the first time when I was seventeen. I played with him in the Disney Team Championship one year when he asked me to play as his partner. To play with Arnold Palmer for seven days straight was amazing. At my very first Masters I got to stay in the Crow's Nest with Tom Watson, played my first round with Jackie Burke, and played my second round with Gene Sarazen. I've played the Masters with Gene Sarazen! I played the first two days of the 1972 U.S. Open with Jack Nicklaus and Julius Boros while in 1973 I played with Ben Crenshaw and Sam Snead. In what other sports can you do that? It was so cool playing with them, and you'd often catch yourself watching them instead of concentrating on your own game. Fortunately, by 1973, I'd played enough golf with Sam that I was comfortable being around him.

****

"I know I am getting better at golf because I am hitting fewer spectators."

Gerald R. Ford

****

People always asked where my aggressive play came from. I think it comes down to the golf courses that I grew up playing. In Richmond, there was this course that had very, very small greens and it wasn't so much that I was aiming for the flag as it was that I just wanted to keep it on the green. I played a terrific Perry Maxwell course at Wake Forest that had very small, undulating greens. You really had to be precise with your irons there. I think it just became habit for me to play at the flag.

Guys on tour do see me as ultracompetitive, but I'm really only playing the way that I play best. [Lee] Trevino and Chi-Chi [Rodriguez] are bantering back and forth all the time while Fuzzy [Zoeller] carries on and talks all the time too. You really have to play the way that best suits you. Hell, my whole generation was ADD! I had to really focus to stay in the game. I think I had to grind it out, and yes, I enjoyed walking the fairways, looking at all the pretty girls, but besides that, I really had to stay focused. I played better mad and mean, but I was doing what worked best for me, and I enjoyed every minute of it. Gosh, I loved to play. Give me a second chance and I'd do it all over again.

I was a very fast player in my day. When I was a commentator on television I would find myself dozing off in the tower as the guys today take so long to hit the ball. Sometimes, I just don't know what the hell they're looking at. I mean, it's right there in front of you, you've got the yardage, you've got the green, and there's the flag, hit it already. It's almost like they've got too many routines, too many things set up by their sports psychiatrists to help them play. It's simply not that tough. When Dan [Pohl] and I used to play, our sports psychiatrist was the local bartender! If you look at the really great players today, do you see a sports psychiatrist with Tiger Woods? I haven't. It makes you kinda wonder. I can't imagine Jack Nicklaus ever using one either. A couple of years ago I was watching the British Open when Greg Norman was making a run for the lead. I remember they had this great shot of Greg Norman and Padraig Harrington heading to the first tee. Padraig was walking with his entourage of four people, you know, trainer, nutritionist, sports psychiatrist, and there was Greg Norman walking with just his caddy. We took care of business, and I mean we took care of it on our own. We didn't have all these people around as a crutch.

If you look at today's players, and you have to be specific about who you're looking at, I believe that the very top two percent of the players are probably playing to win, and I think a lot of the other guys are probably playing to make pay check because there's just so much money out there. When I came on tour we were all playing to win because there wasn't that much money out there. The very first check I ever made was at the Sahara Invitational in Las Vegas in fall 1971, right after Q school, where I tied for ninth and made thirty-three hundred bucks. I tied for third at the Walt Disney World Classic at the Walt Disney World Resort about five weeks later that year and made eight thousand, eight hundred and fifty dollars. Jack Nicklaus won, Deane Beman came in second, and Arnold Palmer and I tied for third. That money got me through the winter; I mean, I was broke.

My very first win on tour was at the Sahara Invitational in Las Vegas in 1972. That prize money was twenty-seven thousand dollars. When I won the PGA Championship in 1977 at Pebble Beach, the prize money was forty-five thousand dollars, and when I won the Players Championship in 1979 at TPC Sawgrass at Ponte Vedra Beach, Florida, it was sixty-three thousand dollars. I look at the millions that they're earning today, and I don't feel one bit of jealousy. Do I wish I'd earned more money playing? Of course I do, but today endorsements are bigger, everything is bigger, and it's a great credit to golf that it has achieved similar status to other sports. I always thought it was wild that some guy could get paid eight million dollars to go hit two twenty-five and make more errors than anyone else at second base or something, but golf has finally achieved what it had set out to achieve.

Mark E. Squire

I tried to never be intimidated by anyone, but I was completely in awe of Tom Weiskopf. I've played with him on numerous occasions, finished runner-up to him in tournaments, and I beat him at Firestone one year. He was such a pretty player to watch, and his ability to craft shots was simply amazing. He made a great statement once after finishing a round at the Masters. He was talking to a reporter and fuming about not doing better. The reporter asked, "What's wrong? What's wrong, big T?" Tom replied, "I'm out there painting pictures, and those guys are scribbling and beating me!" I thought that perfectly described the way Weiskopf played because that's exactly what he did, he painted pictures.

I played with Tom in his first round at Baltusrol one year. He shot a sixty-three, and I'll never forget on the seventeenth hole, a big, long downhill par three, he and his caddy, Leroy, were talking about what club to hit. Leroy was pushing for a three iron to the middle of the green. Tom, who's like two pars from a sixty-four, asked what club to use to get close. Leroy said, "T, you gotta take a two iron and make a little high-cut." Tom replied, "Okay, let's just paint a little high-cut two iron in there." Who the hell hits a high cut two iron, especially when you're in the middle of shooting a sixty-three at a U.S Open? That's something you do on a Tuesday in a practice round. Well, he hit just the perfect shot. I can't remember whether he made the putt for birdie or not, but I stood there with my mouth hanging open. He was really something to watch.

It just occurred to me that Phoenix was one of my favorite places to play. I was the runner-up at the Phoenix Open in my first three appearances there. Lost a playoff to Homero Blancas in 1972, lost by a shot to Bruce Crampton in 1973, and lost by a shot to Johnny Miller in 1974. I finally won it in 1982. That tournament was a staple for me, and I really loved playing there. It was a wonderful place and had great people. It was a sad day when it moved from downtown Phoenix to the Scottsdale TPC.

If I had only one course to play in my life it would have to be Pebble Beach. I already have my foursome picked out, and that would be my two sons, Travis and Tucker, and my son-in-law. I've been lucky enough to have played in that foursome many times, and it's really cool. The last time we were together like that was before Travis went back to Wake Forest. Tucker made a hole in one. Travis was really ticked as Tucker now has three holes in one but Travis doesn't have any. My boys are getting to do things I'd never dreamed of when I was their age. It's really cool to play golf with them.

****

"I would like to deny all allegations by Bob Hope that during my last game of golf, I hit an eagle, a birdie, an elk and a moose."

Gerald Ford

****

I was born in Johannesburg, South Africa, and was the youngest of three kids. When I was eight years old my mother passed away after suffering from cancer. Although my father was often away from home working in the gold mines, he managed to take out a loan and buy me a set of clubs so that I could begin playing golf. I played regularly at the Virginia Park golf course in Johannesburg, and that's where my love affair with golf first began. By age fourteen I was playing my first round of golf, managing to par the first three holes. When I was sixteen, I guess I was extremely confident of my abilities and proclaimed that I would eventually rise to become number one in the world of golf. I turned professional at seventeen.

In 1963, Arnold Palmer, Jack Nicklaus and I were playing in the Canada Cup in Paris. On Sunday night, at the conclusion of that event, we were all going to fly to Melbourne, Australia, to play in the Australian Open at the Royal Melbourne Golf Club. The final round was fogged out, so our travel agent said, "Look, if you leave now I can get you into Royal Melbourne three and a half hours before you play, if you wanna go." Jack said no as he considered the odds of making it remote with all the flight changes that had to be made and was going to stick with his original plans. I, on the other hand, decided to go even though it was a definite risk as it meant taking the rather complicated route of Paris to New York, New York to Los Angeles, Los Angeles to Hawaii, Hawaii to Fiji, Fiji to Sydney and finally, Sydney to Melbourne. I did get there three hours before play was due to start. I'm sure I wouldn't have made it today, not with all the travel delays that go on these days. I had time for a sandwich, a shower and even managed to go hit a few balls before I was due to tee off on a golf course I'd never seen before. I won that Australian Open by seven shots using clubs I'd never played with before.

It was definitely the most amazing win during my career, not the most important, but definitely the most amazing. Although it wasn't the most important win of my career, it is still a hugely important venue. Jack and I used to battle it out to see who could win the most Australian Opens during his career. The competition was extremely fierce, but I came out on top with seven wins while Jack had six. Still, no mean feat by Jack, just one short!

I constantly thought about getting a record number of Australian Opens, and I wondered if I could make it. Getting there is as long a trip as any human can or should make. I think there's a sixteen-hour time difference. By the time I got there, I didn't know if my name was Arthur or Martha, I was absolutely numb from the time change and sitting for that length of time. I was simply playing from memory and it was a miracle I could sink that many puts. It just goes to show you that golf, as the Scottish would say, "is a very strange game, laddie." Another point is that while I thought about getting the most number of Australian Open wins, that one at Royal Melbourne in 1963 was only my third win at that event. I thought about that record from so early on.

I wanted to get married to my now wife, who I'd been going out with since I was fourteen, but I didn't have enough money. We went to Australia, where there was the biggest golf tournament in the world. Prize money for the event was five thousand pounds, which in those days was probably the equivalent to two hundred thousand dollars today. I said to her before the tournament started that if I won, we would get married. The competition was extremely tough, with the top Australians and Americans, as well as players from all over the world in attendance. Anyway, after fifty-four holes I had a four-shot lead, but on the final day the rains came in and delayed things to the next day. That was like the worst torture as I wanted to marry this little chick so badly.

After winning that tournament, which was at the end of November, beginning of December, we got married on January 19, 1957, four years after I turned professional. I had to make sure she didn't like somebody else so I made sure we got married pretty quickly! Prior to the win in Australia, I had made arrangements with her that if we got married, she would pay for the ring. That's how bad it was, the room we stayed in was so small that when you put the key in the keyhole the damn window broke! We've been married for sixty years, and we got remarried at my beach house in South Africa with all of our children and grandchildren watching.

I played the Masters at Augusta in 1961, and led Arnold Palmer by three shots after three rounds. We got rained out on Sunday so the match carried over to Monday. That was simply agonizing. I would be the first international player to win the

Masters, and with this icon Arnold Palmer in the running, everyone was pulling for him. The only ones pulling for me were my wife and my dog!

People always talk about Jack Nicklaus and all the other great players, and I say the greatest gentleman I have ever played with is Jack Nicklaus. He was always so considerate, and after all was said and done, although it's our living, golf is also just a game.

When I've played Augusta through the years, fiftytwo in total, I liken it to a big mousetrap with a giant piece of cheese on it, just waiting for you to take a nibble from the wrong side. I look at number twelve, which should be the easiest hole on the golf course, but people don't realize it's on the low ground on the course and the wind swirls around down there. If you stand on the twelfth tee and look over to the flag on eleventh green, it's right next to you, the wind will be blowing with you. Then you look at the flag on the twelfth green and it's blowing into you. It simply confuses you, and if you take the wrong club you're in the water or over the green. It's the most frustrating hole. It's only an eight iron but goodness me, has that hole ruined or determined the winner of that tournament on many an occasion.

✶✶✶✶✶✶✶✶✶✶✶✶✶✶

"If you are caught on a golf course during a storm and are afraid of lightning, hold up a one iron. Not even God can hit a one iron."

Lee Trevino

✶✶✶✶✶✶✶✶✶✶

If I was to rate the majors in my favor, I would say that the British Open is number one and the Masters is number two. The PGA has the strongest field, but I'd rate the U.S. Open number three and the PGA number four. There's not a lot of difference between the four, but the British Open is the oldest of the majors, it's steeped in such tradition and, you know, it's not an automatic, it's more about instinct. You could be hitting the same shots off the same tees and fairways all week and use a different club each time. You get in a bunker at Augusta and it's all beautifully manicured and it's a relatively easy shot compared to being in a bunker at the British Open when you have to play out backwards. You say to yourself, "This is not very fair." Well golf ain't meant to be fair, laddie!

The man I found that knew the most about a golf swing during my whole career was Ben Hogan. I thought he was the best striker of the ball. I mean, he was so far superior to Tiger Woods, who was on the verge of becoming the best golfer ever.

We're going to see what happens from now on, and I really hope he does well, but Ben Hogan was the best striker I ever saw from tee to green. He never played with perfect bunkers or perfect fairways or perfect greens, and he played with a larger golf ball. I loved to listen to his stories, but the trouble was he only told one story a year, and that was done badly!

Trevino was fantastic, you know, and his happiness was contagious. He always had great stories to tell. This is one of the things I've tried to do with all this traveling around the world, to prioritize all the great stories I've heard. I've done a lot of after-dinner speaking, and it's a wonderful thing to recall all these great stories. You'd better be sure to write them down.

I was born in McKinney, Texas, and I began playing golf at age six. When I was twelve, we moved to Austin, Texas, where my dad joined the Austin Country Club. I was just a kid, but the Austin Country Club had so many singledigit handicap players it was crazy. There were about fifteen to twenty juniors who were a few years older than me, and they were really good. I think they're still playing amateur golf in the Texas area today. Later on, I attended the University of Texas on a golf scholarship and had the chance to play a lot of golf under the Harvey Penick's guidance.

At the time, Ben Crenshaw, who was born in Austin, and I started our lifelong journey of competing against each other, which has carried all the way through to today. We went to different junior and high schools, and when we finally got to the University of Texas it was like, "Man, I'm tired of competing against this guy. I want him on the same team!" When the coach looked at recruiting Ben, I just couldn't wait to have it happen. We had a pretty good run with a couple of national championships in there. It was great to finally compete with him instead of against him.

Mark E. Squire

Harvey Penick obviously had a big influence on both Ben and me. He was very instrumental in both our games and in developing our abilities. I guess Ben and I were almost joined at the hip through all of it, and it was a great blessing to have that opportunity. When Ben won his second Masters in 1995, it was on the heels of Harvey Penick's passing. I was at home at the time, having not yet flown over to Augusta, and was the one who called Ben and told him that Mr. Penick had passed away. Soon after that call, I flew to Augusta and played a practice round there. Then we all flew back with the sports director of ABC at that time and were part of the ceremony to honor Mr. Penick and recognize his great contributions. Ben and I then traveled back to Augusta, and he had that unbelievable run that rewarded him with his second Masters trophy. It was a great tribute to Mr. Penick, for sure.

Harvey Penick's influence on my game has really been a lifelong journey. I could never put all he taught me into one sentence, but there is one piece of advice that sticks with me today. He'd tell his students to go to dinner with good putters. If you think about it, to be a good putter you can't have a crappy attitude. You have to have a great attitude and have high expectations to get good results. Basically, he was telling us to hang out around positive, good, upbeat people who would have a good effect on us and who would be a great influence on our careers and lives. It's way more than just having someone to go to dinner with, for sure. It was a great piece of advice.

I've tried to pass along as much of Mr. Penick's advice as I can to anyone starting out in their first year on tour. I don't feel that today's new players are really taking advantage of the wealth of information and knowledge that the guys who went before them have in their heads. It's disturbing, and I don't quite understand it. When Ben [Crenshaw] and I were starting out on tour, we just couldn't wait to play a practice round with the top players who were older and knew more than we did, whoever it was. I tried to play as many rounds as I could with them, and they were really good to me. I learned a lot from them. Nowadays, I see more and more of these guys surrounded by their own entourages. They have a strength coach, a sports psychiatrist, and a nutritionist. It's almost as if the entourages are trying to protect their own positions with these golfers. They keep their players so isolated that they don't have the opportunity to learn from the golfers who went before them. I think they're really missing out, and it's a shame. The great thing is that we're beginning to see a couple of the younger players realizing that this isn't the way to do it. It was great to see Jordan Spieth taking advantage of Ben Crenshaw's knowledge at the Masters, you know, tapping into the knowledge that's out there ahead of him.

I played a couple of weeks ago, which was at the end of a very poor year for me. I had a lot of distractions with my wife passing away in January after her battle with cancer. Just when I was starting to come back and play well again, I slipped at a Senior PGA tournament and tore my meniscus, so this year has been a bust. I am looking forward to next year and improving my game again. There was a lot of new equipment that came out around the year 2000, but that was at the end of my career with the regular PGA Tour. My first year on the Champions Tour was 2000. For the first five years, I split my time between the PGA Tour and the Champions Tour, as a number of players are doing now, and that was some of the best golf I'd ever played. I was leading in a lot of the statistics and had some good runs during my first two years on the Champions Tour.

Mark E. Squire

Now, I don't think that any of us who grew up in the era of wooden clubs are going to achieve the same benefits that the guys who grew up with the lighter equipment are seeing, but I believe that the new technology we're witnessing does help everyone. It does make the game easier as when you have big-headed clubs hitting balls that don't spin as much you tend to hit straighter shots. The part that concerns me is that the really long hitters have a much greater benefit from the new equipment than Uncle Harry or Aunt Agnes.

I guess I was a bit of a pioneer as I was the first golfer on tour to put three wedges in my bag. Back then, the most loft anyone would use was a fifty-six degree sand wedge, but they still carried two and three irons in their bag. Some guys even carried a one iron. Dave Pelz came to me in 1979, as he had been following some other guys around, and he convinced me that, as good as my short game was, it could be better. He was a strong advocate of having a more lofted club in there, gave me some stats and so forth, and in 1980 I incorporated what he was telling me into my bag. It totally changed my game as well as how everyone set up their bag. In 1981, my first full year with that setup, I was the leading money winner. I'd never finished better than fourteenth on the money list prior to that. I was always consistent, always made the top sixty, but never better than fourteenth. From there, I went a decade and never finished outside the top ten on that money list. It was a great time for me and that extra wedge revolutionized my game. It was a full two to three years before a couple of the others started setting their bag up the same way. Now you don't see anyone without it in their bag.

****

"The golf swing is like a suitcase into which we are trying to pack one too many things."

John Updike

****

One of my proudest moments was when I shot an even-par round of seventy-two to win the 1992 U.S. Open at Pebble Beach. However, I had mixed feelings. To shoot a seventy-two when the stroke average for that day was nearly seventy-nine just shows how difficult a course like Pebble Beach can be when the conditions turn ugly. There was only one score better than seventy-two the entire day. Colin Montgomery got in the clubhouse fairly early and posted a good number while we were out there facing disasters at every hole. In this case, I think you had a situation where the USGA and the PGA, who want to test the golfers as they often do, pushed the course's limit. When the greens are firm and fast and the fairways are tight, and you have a situation where the weather conditions change from what was forecast, then all of a sudden something that was at the edge actually goes over that edge. It happened a few other times, like at Shinnecock Hills on Long Island. I like to look at the other guys who have won at Pebble Beach, guys like Lanny Wadkins, who won the PGA Championship in 1977, Jack Nicklaus, who won his third U.S. Open championship there in 1972, and Tom Watson, who won the U.S. Open in 1982. I won the U.S. Open in 1992, Tiger Woods won the U.S. Open in 2000 and Graeme McDowell won the U.S. Open in 2010. Those are some really nice names to be on a list with!

At the other end of the spectrum, so to say, I remember when we had just moved to Austin, Texas. I was twelve years old, we had joined the Austin Country Club, and I really thought I was a hot shot golfer. We were playing with a couple of juniors on a Saturday afternoon, and Harvey Penick was acting as starter to send us off the back nine. We were up on the tenth tee when all of a sudden a group of members, who were also starting on the back nine, pulled up behind us. They were some real bigwigs in the club you usually only hear about. I was going to show them how good I was. I reared back on the tee shot and made a long back swing, but when I came down on the ball I hit way behind it and left a huge divot in the ground while my club bounced right over the ball. The ball was still sitting there on the tee. I wanted to just crawl into that divot and die! Obviously, during my career there have been more shots that were a lot costlier than that, but as I've grown older I've learned to not be embarrassed by my poor shots but to go on and learn from them.

What I think is so different in golf today, and I think many of the older players feel the same, is that we seem to be lacking the personalities who once filled the courses. Tiger was such a good player, but he didn't give much back, he wasn't approachable. He didn't sign autographs the way Jack [Nicklaus] and Arnold [Palmer] taught all of us to do. He didn't socialize with the gallery who watched and so much admired his great golf game. I am excited to see what the next ten to fifteen years bring to the tour with the likes of Ricky Fowler, Jordan Spieth, Jason Day and Rory McIlroy and guys like that who are not only great players but nice people too.

You can ask anyone, I don't care who it is, Jack Nicklaus, Tiger Woods, Lee Trevino, Arnold Palmer, we've all lost tournaments, let them slip away. We can always look back and wish we'd handled a certain situation differently. I'm fortunate, I've had a good career. I'm pleased. It could have been better, but I suppose it could have been a whole lot worse too. As I said earlier, I played in California a couple of weeks ago, and I've certainly got some work to do to get my game back. But I feel like I'm healthy, and I'm getting my life grounded again.

Mark E. Squire

****

"Golf is a game that is played on a five-inch course - the distance between your ears."

Bobby Jones

****

When I first got on tour I latched on to Dan Pohl, Tom Purtzer, Howard Twitty and a bunch of the Arizona guys. Well, Dan and I, being the sports nuts that we were, used to do a lot of different things, like when we went to the Final Four and had a ball. In Dallas one year, I remember Dan got us tickets, arranged how to get to the venue we were going to, and basically took care of almost everything. It was a blast.

Dan, Joey Rassett and I were playing together at TPC Sawgrass in Florida when we had a rain out. We all decided to go down to the local 7-Eleven and grab a few beverages for our day off. Although play was canceled for the entire day, we did play the course but only with two clubs each. We just grabbed two clubs out of our bags, whatever we thought would work. I picked a four iron and a wedge, and we went out there and played. Dan kept an eye on us and made sure we didn't get into any trouble.

In 2008, when I was asked to be the 2009 Presidents Cup captain, I jumped at the opportunity. Michael Jordan had attended every Presidents Cup and Ryder Cup that I could recall. Obviously, he's missed one or two. I didn't know him that well, but he does a basketball camp for the kids in Santa Barbara where I used to live, so I got to know him a little. One time, out of the blue, I said to him, "Mike, if I'm ever captain of one of these things I want you to be like a special assistant. Would you do that?" Michael kinda laughed and replied, "Sure, sure."

So, when I was asked to be captain of the 2009 Presidents Cup team I called him right away and said, "Hey Michael, I've just accepted the position of captain for the 2009 Presidents Cup team and I'm going to ask you to be my assistant." He replied, Yeah, yeah, yeah!" I said, "Okay, I can tell you the dates now. Tomorrow morning, I'm going on the Golf Channel so, you know, I need to know tonight." There was a very short pause, and then he said, "I'll be there." The players were pretty excited. I really like Sean O'Hair and I was texting him a lot and calling him. When he told me he was coming in early for the event I said to him, "I'm playing Monday with Michael, the course is closed, and Michael wants to play a round with you and Hunter Mahan." Well, Sean was just like a four year old! He was so excited.

I think, and it's just my opinion, that this may be the only time I captain a team, but I think it will be great to have Michael there. I really enjoy him, he's a golf freak, and if I was leading a British Open after the third round or something, you know, trying to stomach that on Saturday night, I would want to have dinner with someone like Michael Jordan versus Jack Nicklaus or Arnold Palmer. He would know how to deal with that sort of pressure. Michael texts me all the time, and while nine out of ten texts are pretty normal, pretty strong, every now and then he'll send me something and I'll go, "Holy cow, that was deep!" To have someone who's dealt with those situations, those highpressure moments, on the team, it's a unique perspective for some of the younger players. To get his take on how he'd deal with it will be different for them for sure. Someone of that caliber giving his experiences of dealing with pressure situations, how much better can it get than Michael Jordan? The one word that sums up Michael Jordan is that he's a winner.

I just felt like instead of Davis Love III with us, and I spoke to Davis about the situation and he completely understood, having someone who's won the way Michael has consistently won was really important. Michael's sent me texts about how nervous he was about it. He knows he's never done anything like this before. I laughed, but every guy on the team, they were all tickled pink that he was going to be there. One of the guys has a poster that showed John Starks dunking over Michael Jordan, but he's really dunking over Horace Grant and Michael is on the side. Well, they blew that up even bigger, and it's the first thing you'll see when you walk into the team room. So, we're going to beat up on him a little, for sure. It's not like it's just going to be all laughs, he'll get beat up on just like any other player.

Mark E. Squire

I've got a small short list of embarrassing things that have happened to me during my career. For example, right there in the great town of Scottsdale, Arizona, I hit a shrimp hook, I think in the first playoff hole against Sandy Lyle, that landed left of the water on the eighteenth hole and trickled back into the water. I was also at Hilton Head one year, playing with Tom Watson in the last group on this little par three, I think it was the fourteenth hole, and the wind was howling. It was normally a seven iron shot, but because of the wind I found I had to hit a five. Well, I hit that ball so fat that I bounced it into the water right in front of me! If it happens twenty years into your career you can turn around and laugh it off, but when you're struggling to win your first tournament that can really screw you up. When you get embarrassed in golf, and it happens a lot, there's missed two-footers, there's pulled shots, but if you escape out of bounds or a hazard you don't look so bad. I rarely escaped those. I've had a lot of re-tees in my career! The most embarrassing shots are those you make and they don't even look like a golf shot, you just want to fall back into a big black hole and disappear.

My game is either good or bad, and it's no longer consistent, so I will tell you that at times I can get a little sharp, quick, or smart assed, whatever the right words are. I get a little frustrated when I'm ready to play an event and, for example, I've got to go from somewhere to Washington, D.C. to do a press conference, and then go somewhere else to do another PR event. I just want to go and play golf. When it came to the Presidents Cup I wanted my players to be relaxed when they had to play. We didn't want to have to put on a tie or go to another opening or dinner, so Greg Norman and I tried to beat the holdup a little bit. We did the same sort of things, but we did them at a faster pace, got our guys in and out of there so they could relax for the week.

I've had some very, very good tournaments, and that makes it fun. I get most happy when my friends do well on the PGA Tour and I know why that is. I love to play golf but I'm not a rah-rah type of guy. I don't go out and get in my players' faces, screaming and yelling, but I get intense in watching them compete. So in the Ryder Cups and Presidents Cups I went out and I stared, and I watched what everyone did. That's always going to be the best fun for me.

I did have a special job for my caddy, Joe LaCava, at the Presidents Cup. I asked him to take care of all the other caddies and to make sure they had whatever they needed. He also had to watch Anthony Kim, the young, loud man, as we called him. Kim is a great, great player who likes to have fun, and I joked with Joe that I had everyone else figured out but he was in charge of Anthony Kim. Joe replied, "You got it."

****

"Golf can best be defined as an endless series of tragedies obscured by the occasional miracle."

Author Unknown

****

Well, as you all probably know, I was born in Shreveport, Louisiana, and graduated from the University of Arkansas in 1954. I turned professional four years later and won my first PGA Tour event in 1964 at the Cajun Classic Open Invitational at Oakborne Country Club in Lafayette, Louisiana. Although I didn't win any majors on the regular PGA Tour, my twenty-four wins on the Senior PGA Tour, as it was called then, resulted in me capturing five Senior Tour majors, including three U.S. Senior Opens in 1982, 1984, and 1985. When I was in Phoenix for the Phoenix Open, which I won in 1971 and 1978, I played against such golf greats as Arnold Palmer, Don January, Gene Littler, and Johnny Miller. Believe me, they were amazing golfers to play with. I'm great with faces, and I can see them now, but I'm not so good with names. Hell, if you asked me what I had for breakfast this morning I wouldn't be able to tell you!

I think that today's players are fun guys but in a different way. I came from a group of guys who were not only great competitors but who also weren't afraid to just sit around and tell stories. All the entertainers were around in my day, you know, with the Bing Crosby Clambake and occasions like that that meant so much to golf in general. Now it's just a crying shame to see a tournament like the Bob Hope [Desert Classic] or the Bing Crosby Clambake lose their names and identities. I don't know why these big companies don't simply call it the Bob Hope Desert Classic sponsored by Humana. The same with the AT&T, they could have done exactly the same and kept the history of the tournament alive. Those guys were giants in our day. Bob Hope and Bing Crosby, oh my gosh, they helped start golf, professional golf if you want to put it that way. If it hadn't been for those guys I don't know if we'd be sitting here today. They were such great gentlemen, and we all had our own great memories of them. At least I did!

****

"I'm not saying my golf game went bad, but if I grew tomatoes, they'd come up sliced."

Miller Barber

****

It does hurt me to see the Bob Hope Desert Classic and the Bing Crosby Clambake tournaments fade away. I mean, I got to play in them for many years, and I have so many great memories from both of those tournaments. I consider myself extremely fortunate to have met both Bob Hope and Bing Crosby, and I got to stay with Bob Hope at the Desert Classic in Palm Springs. I've got this little story about Bing Crosby where I was teamed with Harvey Warwick. We were playing Spyglass at Pebble Beach in, I believe, 1967, the first year the course was opened. Well, we go around there and my card shows I've shot a sixtyone even though it felt like a little more than that. I'll never forget going into the clubhouse and saying to Harvey, "We'd better check this scorecard very carefully here, I don't want any screw-ups." Needless to say, the guy who scored our card forgot to enter the scores from the last hole, the eighteenth! Well, it was too late. Next day, the local San Francisco newspaper had the headline "Barber-Warwick Error" in big bold print. I'll never forget that, and I thought we had a chance of winning that tournament.

After that happened, it would have been easy to just disappear, but we both went out the next day for the round at the Cypress course, where we met up with Bing Crosby. He was really nice to us, said he appreciated us coming out to play that day, and agreed that some players wouldn't have done that after the big newspaper headline. He turned to us and said, "Anytime you two want to play in the Bing Crosby Clambake tournament, you've got a spot." I replied, "Thank you so much, Mr. Crosby. I certainly appreciate that." After that incident, I attended the tournament for a number of years and played with some great guys. You really had some great characters back in my day, it was simply a different era. Although the Bing Crosby Clambake was a tournament you'd still want to win, you were also out there to have fun and socialize with these fellas. We were shown a good time, and that's what we used to do.

When I go back and look at some of the golf clubs we used to play with in those days, I say to myself, "My gosh, how in the world did I even manage to hit that ball as well as I did with those clubs?" That's the interesting thing about the guys of my era, if you made us younger again and put us in the present day with the current crop of golfers and with the latest equipment, we'd still be some of the best golfers out there simply because we were some of the best ball strikers on tour. I was taught by some of the great players. Jackie Burke was one of my tutors while Julius Boros, Don January and all those guys, they all helped me. I'll never forget what Jackie told me one time. He said, "Miller, when you go out and play, don't go and play with somebody you can beat. Go play with somebody who can beat you and learn what the hell they're doing." So I did a lot of that and got to be good friends with all of those great players. Like Jackie told me, if you show a little humility these guys will help you. I was very fortunate in that I could do that and have all those great players teach me the game of golf. As I've already said, I don't think I'd be sitting here today if it wasn't for all the great help those guys gave me. My hat's off to all of them, and it always will be.

The Phoenix Open tournament that was held at Phoenix Country Club will always be special for me because, when you go back and look at those courses, you realize the modern courses are nothing like them, they're nothing like this Phoenix Country Club course. It's great to come back to the older golf courses that require good ball striking, not just getting on the tee and hitting the fire out of the ball. You had to know how to maneuver the ball around the course. I've always enjoyed playing that type of golf because that's what the game used to be. Today, they just whack it three hundred yards down the fairway, get down there and just whack it again! Ha! I wish I could do that today.

Byron Nelson, one of the greatest players of our time, and Louise, his wife, lived in Texarkana, Arkansas. They would drive through where I grew up on their way to the Masters every year. Mr. Nelson would practice on our local course, and Mr. Murphy, the club professional, would come and get me out of school to caddy for him. I made fifty cents a day and a dime tip if I had a great day and didn't lose any of his golf balls. I was just beginning to play a little golf back then, though I didn't know too much, but over the course of the three days I caddied for Mr. Nelson, I noticed every now and then that he did exactly the same thing. It's a terrible thing to say, but he had a shank! It's a terrible word, and I shouldn't have mentioned it, but finally I got up the courage to ask Mr. Nelson, "Why in the world . . . why, why?" He cut me off right there and replied, "Miller, I can't tell you why I do that, but in every round of professional golf I've ever played I've shanked a ball every now and then." I said, "Well, that's a feat in itself if you can shank all these balls and still win as many tournaments as you have. That's something special." He just smiled at me. I saw him shank a ball, and he was very sincere about it. I was in total awe when I watched him play. When I became a little more knowledgeable about golf I realized what it must have taken to overcome something like that.

Many, many years ago my grandmother said to me, "Miller, you're going to go out and meet all these people and it's just as easy to say, 'Yes, sir' or 'No, sir' or 'Yes, ma'am' or 'No, ma'am' as it is to say 'Uh huh' or 'What,' like some of these kids today. These kids don't know what it's all about." I have some of the nicest friends because of my manners. They used to say, "Miller, you've got the best manners, and your kids have the best manners of kids we've ever had around. How do you do that?" So I'd tell them that story of my grandmother teaching me how to be polite. My kids have the same manners today, otherwise I'd hit them right upside their heads!

Mark E. Squire

****

"Golf is an awkward set of bodily contortions designed to produce a graceful result"

Tommy Armour

****

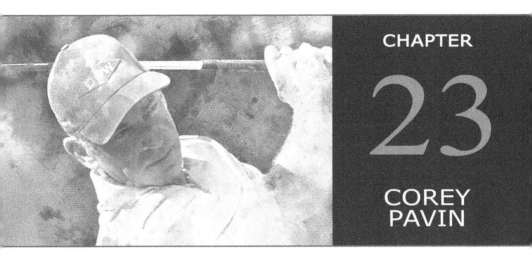

As far as the term "Rain Delay" is concerned, I really feel that the start to my professional golfing career suffered its own "Rain Delay", if you will. This happened by me not getting on the [PGA] Tour, as I thought I would, and it makes a pretty good story. I don't know exactly how many people really paid attention to what happened back then, or what that was all about, but it turned out to be quite the experience.

I turned pro in September of 1982 and, you know, I'd had a good career as an amateur and a college player too. I was thinking to myself that I'd just go off to Q-School [Qualifying School], make it through there with no real issues, go straight on tour and off I go on my golfing career.

So I went to my first Q-School, and back then there were actually two, a Regional and a National level. First you went to the Regional Q-School, and after getting through there, you went to the National Q-School where the top 50 players would get their PGA Tour cards.

I went to the Regional event, which was held in Southern California, and I missed qualifying for the National level, which was a real shock to my system! I had it all planned out that I would be playing on the PGA Tour in 1983. I would just go through the Q-Schools and that would be that. I didn't even make it through the first round of qualifying, let alone the National level, and it was a real shock to say the least.

Of course, I had no "Plan B". There was never a fallback plan. I figured I'd go right through this qualifying process with no problem, when suddenly, there was a real problem! I had to come up with something and back then there was no Web.com Tour. There wasn't a secondary tour in the United States to play on at that time. There were a couple of Mini Tours but I really didn't want to go that route, playing on little 2-day events. I wanted to play tournament golf, full 4-day events.

While I was doing some research and trying to figure out what I was going to do, and I'm talking to all these different people, the one thing they were all saying to me was to go down and play in South Africa. You could fly down there, play in a 1-day qualifying event on the Monday, and if you get through, you'd be playing in the first tournament. If you do well and make the cut in that first tournament you automatically qualify for the next [tournament], and you just keep going, on what I remember was an 8-week tour.

I had this sponsor, an individual, and we had our own deal figured out. I flew out of Los Angeles, down to South Africa, and started playing Tournament golf. I qualified for the first event and found myself playing with the likes of Bob Tway and George Cadle from the US, Nick Price and David Frost from South Africa, as well as a few notable Australians. The first event was played in Sun City, just a regular tour event, and I finished behind David Frost and Nick Price, not quite sure exactly where, but I made the cut.

By default, I found myself playing the following week in the South African PGA Tournament, which was held at The Wanderers in Johannesburg. I actually won that tournament with Nick Price finishing second. I played that last day with Nick and everybody knew who he was. It was pretty cool to find myself playing alongside a guy like that, let alone beating him. After that day we ended up forging a really nice relationship and we've been friends ever since.

As it turned out, I finished up playing six events, finished third on the money list, and by finishing in the top four, I think it was at that time, it gave me my playing privileges in Europe.

I came back home to the United States in February that year and played a couple of events, which included qualifying and playing in The US Open, as well as playing under a sponsor exemption at Bay Hill. At the end of June I flew off to Europe and played there for some three anda-half months, competing against the likes of Bernhard Langer and Seve Ballestero. Seve was just becoming very, very well known world-wide, particularly after winning The Masters in 1980. Nick Faldo, Sandy Lyle and Sam Torrance, as well as some Australians, were also there and I found myself playing against some very stiff competition. We all got along really well and a lot of us became, and still are today, very good friends.

My first tournament in Europe was The Scandinavian Enterprise Open, since 1991 known as the Scandinavian Masters, in which I finished third behind winner Sam Torrance from the UK and, as I recall, Wayne Grady from Australia. About a month or so later, at the end of July that year, I won the Lufthansa

German Open, held at the Cologne Golf and Country Club, by three strokes over Seve Ballesteros, and it was a great confidence booster for me. I went over and played well in South Africa and followed it up by playing well in Europe, competing and beating some of the best players in the world.

As I look back at all these events now, and the path my golf career initially took, I remember saying to myself, "Oh my gosh, the world's coming to an end! I didn't get my card. What am I going to do?" I remember how lost I felt at that time when, in retrospect, it was the best thing that ever happened to me. You think that everything is horrible, nothing is going the way you planned, and that maybe someone else out there has a plan that's better than yours. It makes you think that things really do happen for a reason, I truly believe that.

I was pretty upset at not getting my card, or even getting through the Regionals the first time. I was confused and a bit lost as to what to do next. Smarter minds prevailed, however, and pointed me to playing overseas. It turned out to be one of the best things I could have ever done. I got a great taste of travelling to, and playing golf in, so many different countries, all with their different cultures. I really couldn't have had a better experience. I always look forward to playing tournaments all over the world now, and I'm sure that the experiences I had in South Africa and Europe only helped me enjoy the travelling even more.

To be able to go overseas, to travel and see the world, which is what I've always wanted to do, and to be able to play against and beat some of the best golfers in the world, it doesn't get any better than that! I remember Seve Ballesteros coming up to me after he won at the Trophee Lancôme at Saint-Nom-la-Bretèche in 1983 and saying to me, "Now we're even. You beat me in Germany and I beat you here!"

It really was a blessing in disguise. If I hadn't missed not getting my card that first time, I would never have met these amazing people or enjoyed such great experiences. Things really do happen for a reason.

When I eventually returned Stateside in October of that year I was full of confidence. I went back to the Regional Q-School, made it through there and onto the National Q-School where I received my PGA Tour card. In only my second tournament as a PGA Tour player, the 1984 the Phoenix Open, held at Phoenix Country Club, I finished second and assured myself of my card for 1985. In only my second tournament as a PGA Tour player I was already in the top 125 for the next year.

The beginning of my golf career really was quite the "Rain Delay" for me!

In 2008 I was honored to be named captain of the 2010 US Ryder Cup Team and it's an experience I'll never have in my life again. I can play all the tournaments I like, but to be a Ryder Cup captain was such a great responsibility and I feel extremely honored to have been able to do that.

The Ryder Cup, held at Celtic Manor Resort in Newport, Wales that year, was an extremely close event with the final result of fourteen and-a-half to thirteen and-a-half points in favor of the Europeans. We were subjected to a rain delay, I think, on the Friday which really put us behind the eight ball, only for it to rain again on the Sunday causing us to finalize play on the Monday.

I was really liking the way the matches were stacked up against each other when the pairings came out on that last day.

We were in a position where we could make a great comeback and make history, and we almost did! The crowds were very enthusiastic when play started that day as the Europeans had a four point lead, which is extremely difficult to come back from. However, as the day progressed, it got quieter and quieter and when you got down to the last few matches you could hear a pin drop out there.

The crowds were getting so nervous, so anxious with the turn of events. It really was fun. Obviously, I'd have preferred to have that extra half a point, but it was a great experience being captain and I had a blast all week. To be a Ryder Cup captain is so rare, I'll never come close to feeling the way I did that week.

What I'm most proud of with regards to that Ryder Cup, is that the guys hung in there. They rallied and tried to come back, and although we didn't quite make it, in the press conference that followed it was obvious that the players had each other's backs up on the podium. There was some great dialogue, with Phil Mickelson and Jim Furyk having some great things to say. That was one of my main things, for the entire week, was that we had each other's backs and that we were a team. We win as a team and we lose as a team. Whatever happens, we're a team.

I, like any other pro golfer out there, have had my embarrassing moments on the golf course. The one I recall most readily took place at the 1984 Suntory World Match Play Championship, held at the West Course of Wentworth Golf Club, in Virginia Water, England. I received an invitation to play in this pretty prestigious event in the UK, so I flew in to Heathrow Airport, London early one morning after flying all night. I knew that if I went to sleep I'd never get adjusted to the time difference so I decided to go straight to the golf course.

That Tuesday morning I headed to the first tee, without warming up or hitting any balls on the range, where I took a couple of practice swings before teeing the ball up. There were about twenty to thirty people or so gathered around that slightly elevated first tee. I stepped up, took a swing, and just cold-topped it! I topped it probably not even thirty yards and believe me, it was a solid top. Now some spectators might have known me from when I played in Europe the year before, but still, they were probably saying to themselves, "Who is this guy? This guy's playing in the tournament!"

It was a brilliant top as they'd say over there, and it was pretty embarrassing, but at least I had the excuse that I'd been flying and not slept all night! All I could think of was that these people were certainly not expecting me to play in the tournament!

****

"If you drink, don't drive. Don't even putt."

Dean Martin

****

CPSIA information can be obtained
at www.ICGtesting.com
Printed in the USA
LVHW010910011218
598888LV00050B/2230